THE
MASTER KEY TO ASIA

THE
MASTER KEY TO ASIA

A 6-STEP GUIDE TO UNLOCKING NEW MARKETS

DAVID CLIVE PRICE

Cover design and formatting www.bookstyle.co.uk

Printed by CreateSpace

All enquiries to david@davidcliveprice.com

First published, 2013

ISBN 978-0-9576928-0-0

In memory of my mother,

Muriel Emily Price,

27 June 1923 - 16 September 2012,

who loved travel and life

PRAISE

Savvy and concise from an Asian Master
'*The Master Key to Asia is the right book at the right time about the right areas of the world for many businesses and businesspeople.*

There has been so much nonsense written about doing business in Asia, that it is refreshing to come across a short how-to guide that touches on the most important aspects of managing relationships, cultural pitfalls and expectation management. David correctly gives the theory and cultural relativism a miss preferring to concentrate on what actually happens at the coalface. And he should know. Having spent most of his career advising senior Asian CEOs, pitching for business in Asia, writing about Asian businesses and running his own consultancy from Hong Kong, Taiwan and the Philippines - he is eminently placed to provide this useful primer. Concise, savvy and very helpful. I will recommend it to my clients.'

Mark Dailey, Strategic Communications Consultant, Madano Partnership UK

Guide to feel comfortable and confident in Asia
'*Drawing from a wealth of experience in Asia, David Clive Price has written an easy to navigate book that guides business people or entrepreneurs though the complex maze of Asian cultures. Offering valuable information on business practices, social behaviours, ethics, and religion, this book delves deeper into Asian*

cultures and helps you understand the 'why' so you can feel comfortable and confident interacting with others as quickly as possible. It is a must for any international business professional. It's great also for students who want "real" information about Asian cultures. I highly recommend this book.'

Kara Ronin, Director Executive Impressions, US and France

How not to be a barbarian at the gates
'David Clive Price really knows his Asia. He has toured, lived and worked in just about every corner of it, so he speaks from a wealth of personal experience. Better than that, he possesses the talents of a skilled negotiator and mediator. There can be no better guide to preparing the newcomer to this culturally rich and diverse region for the task of dealing with Asians on a business level. And preparation is the key to this process, for the novice has first to know who and what he is up against, and what to expect of the encounter. The Master Key to Asia is essential reading for those about to knock on Asia's door - if they are to avoid being seen as barbarians at the gates.'

Peter Moss OBE, Director of Government Information Services, Hong Kong (retired)

THE Business Travel Guide for Asia
'David Price has, through his long and enlightened journey across Asia, acquired an impressive amount of anecdotes, experiences, knowledge, wisdom and "cultural insider information", which he generously

and frankly shares (to the extent of sometimes sharing with us personal details) in this Reference Book. Being myself a Japan business expert, I do fully agree with the author's advices & tips, and I do personally think that, especially in Japan & Asia, business and culture are widely connected.

Starting by explaining the basics/fundamentals of Asian Business Culture (patience, long-term relationships, face saving, family-ownership, trust building), David Clive Price then refines his analysis by delivering an outstanding country-by-country overview, which makes this book really UNIQUE. Indeed, there are many books out there covering specific topics about specific countries of Asia (I am the author of one of them), but a well-written & well-thought Guide to a dozen of Asian countries is a rare TREAT!! That is why I recommend this masterpiece, this "Bible of Asian Cross-cultural Communication", without reserve.'

Philippe Huysveld, Director Global Business & Management Consulting, France

A great resource for intercultural organizational communication tactics

'As a student at Rowan University studying communication studies, I've taken a vast interest in intercultural communication. This book provides great detail on how to communicate in intercultural business settings. I was surprised at how much information this book holds!'

Keith Du Barry, Graduate student, New Jersey, US

West meets East

*'I found this book really helpful for looking at the
cultures of East and West from both ends of the
spectrum, especially in relation to business. The format
is clear, and the author's tone is inspiring and helpful.
There are also some intriguing stories and humorous
comments to make the lessons easily digestible. There's
no doubt there's a need for books like this, especially
with so many different Asia cultures to consider. In
fact, I would have liked a bit more on each country
(China, Japan, Malaysia etc.), but since this is first
in the series, I guess that's in the pipeline. Overall,
I would say buy this book if you want to develop
business in Asia and build up your Asia skills.'*

Simon Dowell, Business Development Manager, UK &
Hong Kong

Master Key Master

*'This book is a great guide to learning how business
in conducted in Asia, and how each of the region's
cultures and markets are subtly, but significantly
different. It's full of the author's deep knowledge of
Asia culture and business, has action points that make
the lessons learned easy to implement, and provides a
clear and innovative system for taking your business
in Asia to a whole new level. I'd certainly recommend
it to newcomers and to those already there.'*

Douglas George, Producer 'The Money Programme',
TVB Pearl Hong Kong

ABOUT THE AUTHOR

DAVID CLIVE PRICE is an author, speaker and consultant on Asia's business practices and cultures. For many years he has travelled the region writing about its richly diverse peoples, traditions, beliefs and history.

In 1995, he took up the post of Executive Speechwriter for Asia for the HSBC Group in preparation for Hong Kong's reversion to Chinese sovereignty in 1997. After the 'handover', he set up his own company in Hong Kong, writing presentations and advising companies on their strategic communications in China and in Asia as a whole. His experience with many Asia-wide multinationals gave him the idea of marrying his business experience with his knowledge of Asian cultures.

'It occurred to me that I had something unique to offer to companies entering the Asian market or expanding in the region: not just inside knowledge of how Asian companies operate at the highest level, but also of the countries and cultures in which they operate. I was a travel writer in business class, or (more often) a businessman in coach class, scribbling ideas and notes for books while preparing investor presentations and attending business meetings. Why not share my knowledge and help others on the road to success?'

The result was a stream of books on Asia, including *Within the Forbidden City*, *Travels in Japan*, *The Food of Korea*, *Buddhism: the Fabric of Life in Asia*, *Neon City: Hong Kong*, *The Scent of India*, and *Moonlight over Korea*. Now he has published *The Master Key to Asia* for those companies, business owners and entrepreneurs that want to understand Asia and its many cultures and traditions better as a means to optimize their business operations, maximize their revenue growth and build brand recognition in new markets.

www.davidcliveprice.com

www.facebook.com/davidcliveprice

www.twitter.com/davidcliveprice

www.youtube.com

CONTENTS

AUTHOR'S NOTE

As a special thank you for purchasing this book, please enjoy my free bonus gift: **'Asian Communication and Culture Cheat Sheet'**, which is available at my companion website http://davidcliveprice.com/the-master-key-to-asia-book-gift/. You can also find a wealth of other information and resources on the site. I hope the following will be of great value to you. Please be kind and review this book on Amazon.

Other Books on Asia by David Clive Price

Moonlight Over Korea, Amazon Paperback and Kindle 2012

The Scent of India by Pier Paolo Pasolini, translated by David Clive Price, Amazon Paperback and Kindle 2012

Buddhism: The Fabric of Life in Asia, Formasia Books 2008

Within the Forbidden City, Formasia Books 2004

Neon City Hong Kong, Cameraman 2002

The Food of Korea, Periplus Editions 2002

Travels in Japan, Olive Press 1987

For a full-sized, full-colour version of the books with description, and to order copies, simply go to http://www.davidcliveprice.com/booksonasia/

"There is a missing twenty per cent of human behaviour about which neoclassical economics can give only a poor account. As Adam Smith well understood, economic life is embedded in social life, and it cannot be understood apart from the customs, morals, and habits of the society in which it occurs. In short, it cannot be divorced from culture." (Francis Fukuyama, *Trust, the Social Virtues and the Creation of Prosperity*, 1995)

PREFACE

THE MASTER KEY TO ASIA aims to offer an essential business guide to Asian economic life and the diverse societies in which it is based. Understanding Asia better through enhanced cultural awareness is the key to business success and to the professional development and personal confidence that drives that success.

Performance is largely results driven in the West. Many business people wanting to launch in Asia wonder why they should learn a lot of 'touchy feely' stuff about culture. In their eyes, they are up to speed on operations and nuts-and-bolts issues. What else is there? They think it's better to arrive, make some deals and worry about the finer points later.

They are wrong. Cultural awareness goes beyond knowledge of when to take your shoes off or how to use chopsticks or say 'hello' and goodbye' in the local language. Without a basic understanding of how Asia business culture works, or any willingness to learn, they often make mistakes that can set back or destroy their business plans altogether. It would be far better to invest in cultural understanding at the outset.

This book is intended for those companies and solo entrepreneurs that want to invest time and resources in Asia for the long run. Not only those who are preparing to enter the markets there, but those who are already there and developing their platform, those who are headquartered or based in more 'Western' and cosmopolitan cities like Hong Kong and Singapore and plan to expand, and those in core Europe, Britain,

America, Canada, Australia and New Zealand that see Asia and its diverse economies and cultures as the key to future success in the global economy.

INTRODUCTION

WELCOME AND THANK YOU for choosing to read this book. I hope you will find it a wise investment, for it is an investment both in yourself and in the future of your business.

As the centre of the world's economic gravity moves towards the East, there could not be a better time for unlocking and developing new markets nor a more urgent need to rise to the challenge of growth, innovation and personal development that these emerging markets present. In the midst of economic uncertainty in the West, more and more people are looking for new opportunities and strategies that lie beyond their familiar horizons.

No other region on earth has caught the attention of global businesses so much as rapidly expanding Asia. China is poised to become the world's leading economy. The emerging markets of Asia have GDP growth rates that are the envy of the West. The region has the world's largest, most affluent, and most rapidly expanding middle class. The list of economic achievements and attractions is unending.

Now more than ever there is a need for companies outside the region, or those fortunate enough to already have a foothold in one or more Asian economies, to develop their presence, pursue opportunities and create long-term relationships with their potential Asian partners, suppliers, customers and investors.

As Francis Fukayama (quoting Adam Smith) declared in the quotation that begins this book, "economic life is embedded in social life, and it cannot be understood apart from the customs, morals, and habits of the society in which it occurs. In short, it cannot be divorced from culture."

Nowhere is this truer than in Asia. Understanding the cultures of Asia beyond India, which include the business practices, business etiquettes, social and familial behaviours, approach to ethics, cultural traditions and spiritual beliefs of the region as a whole as well as of individual countries, is vital to business success.

The Master Key to Asia is written specially for those entrepreneurs, companies and business owners that want to quickly find their feet or develop their footprint in this fascinating and complex region, home to potentially the largest but also the most diverse 'consumer class' on earth. The easy-to-follow chapters provide a logical roadmap so that you can find your way in a business culture that may seem daunting at first. However, Asia offers increasing rewards to those that stick to the path and accept the need to learn new rules and approaches.

Asia is by no means a homogenous region. However, there are customs and attitudes that are common to almost all countries that lie beyond India (not included in this book because it is a book in itself) and are bounded by Japan to the east, China to the north and the Philippines to the south. These customs and cultures mark Asia out as unique.

Doing business in Asia is different to doing business anywhere else in the world, largely because of the special emphasis placed on 'indirect' and 'intangible' values such as building credibility, relationships and trust rather than on immediate business returns and bottom lines.

That said, there are also fascinating and subtle differences in the way individual Asian countries approach these 'intangibles' based on their respective cultural and religious beliefs. This inevitably results in some marked differences in management attitudes from country to country.

For example, top management in China understands their business world very differently to their counterparts in Japan or Korea, and all of them may have different expectations of a partner from core Europe, Britain, America and Australasia. At the same time, each member of the business community across Asia cherishes certain cultural and social beliefs that they expect the foreign partner to make some attempt to grasp.

The master key to doing business in Asia is to gain an adequate *understanding* not only of the region's business assumptions and cultures as a whole but also those of the individual countries that makes up Asia's colourful patchwork quilt. By *understanding* I mean more than doing research. I mean acknowledging that you have your own cultural style and approach, which is rooted in your education and upbringing. This ingrained assumption that there is only one (largely Western) way of doing things is very difficult to shake off.

But unless you are ready to recognize the differences between your personal and professional style and that of the business community of the new market in which you are aiming to succeed, you will never fully unlock the markets of the region.

Building new business in the dynamic and diversified economies of Asia is an enormous challenge. It requires confidence. It requires the courage to learn new viewpoints while re-assessing your own. It requires the flexibility to change and accept change. It requires a willingness to develop new aspects of yourself and your business as well as a sense of 'other' perspectives.

In other words, if you want to learn the secrets of success that lie within Asia's economies, you have to discover how to turn the master key in the lock and push the door open. That master key is culture, and business culture above all.

Who should read this book
There are four main groups of people that will benefit from reading this book:

- Firstly, companies, business owners and entrepreneurs planning entry or developing their business in one or more markets in the Asia region. They will need a clear plan of action for understanding essential cross-cultural differences within and between countries, applying general principles and lessons learned to specific business operations such as working, meeting, communicating, relationship building, networking and negotiating with clients, partners and colleagues from different cultures.

- Secondly, business leaders that want to develop their cross-cultural leadership skills and exhibit appropriate behaviour to project confidence, commitment, sincerity, positivity, sensitivity and wisdom across cultures, as well as genuine interest in and passion for the culture and beliefs of their host countries. This includes developing presentational skills, ability to deliver inspiring and motivational speeches, hosting dinners and events, and being a guest at banquets.

- Thirdly, CEOs and senior executives that manage cross-cultural teams that operate in the Asia region, building their confidence to recognise and handle cross-cultural issues in the workplace as well as to provide them with the skills to build strong work relationships, create trust and build respect and credibility across borders.

- And fourthly, all those that regard the discovery of new cultures as being an essential journey for expanding their own horizons, improving their ability to interact with and understand other people and their beliefs, and that never want to stop learning or developing themselves. Respecting other cultures provides food for the soul and stimulation for the mind. Crucially, it breeds confidence and confidence breeds success.

STEP ONE

THE CONFIDENCE FACTOR

WHEN I FIRST CAME TO ASIA, I was pretty much down and out. I didn't have a job, I had split with my partner of 12 years, and I didn't have the courage to sell the farmhouse that we had part-shared in Italy while I wrote my first novel and tried to be self-sufficient as a wine and olive farmer. I wasn't ready to go back to recession-bound Britain with my tail between my legs. So I hit on the idea of starting some sort of business in Asia, possibly related to travel or import/export.

I didn't have much business experience, except for selling the olive harvest by the demi-john at the local olive press each year, and writing the occasional paid feature or article. Above all, I didn't know much about Asia except what I had read in novels and travel books.

And yet the country I chose was possibly one of the most culturally challenging in Asia: Japan. Very little English was spoken in Japan at that time outside Tokyo (and often inside Tokyo), and although I found the country's complex traditions often fascinating, as a foreigner with only a superficial acquaintance with Japanese ways I was at best tolerated. Of course I made friends, I made contacts, I tried out some business ideas. I could just about cover the rent. But the curious thing was that the more I learned about the country and its culture, the more I spoke some basic Japanese the less I seemed to make any progress. There was something missing.

It was only when I moved on to Hong Kong after a year in a love-hate relationship with Japan that I realized what that something missing was. Confidence.

Hong Kong at that time was a Chinese city but with British characteristics. Although I hated myself for thinking it, that British element was enough to get me into the Chinese world to such an extent that I ended up marrying a local Chinese and becoming part of a very extended Chinese family. As a result, I got to know all kinds of Chinese traditions and ways (for example, you don't take an apple from the pyramid of apples at the table for ancestor worship!), and the more I was accepted because I knew how to behave the more my confidence rose. I was still broke; or rather we were still broke. But I had a family around me, a promise of long-term relationships and support, and I had a strong incentive to be more ambitious.

Confidence, local knowledge and long-term intentions are essential to building a successful business in Asia. That is a central message of this book. They take time to show results, but those results are well worth waiting for.

It took me another few years in Hong Kong, dotted with successes and failures, for me to learn this. I was stubborn. I was still hooked on the dream of writing books more than taking a salaried job in a company and supporting my spouse and myself. I still didn't have the courage to take the leap into the professional world.

It was only when I was down and out for the second time, this time unable to sleep in a walk-up one-bedroom apartment above a noisy nightclub in Hong Kong's entertainment district, that it occurred to me that I had skills that could be taken to another level. I had studied the history of ideas at university. I had a Ph.D. I could write. I could speak come Cantonese, Japanese, even Korean. I had published two or three travel books about Asia.

The problem was that I was not applying any of this knowledge and competence systematically. I was not digging deep enough to develop my talents. I was not using my cultural confidence in any meaningful or consistent way. *Wake up and smell the coffee!* I told myself.

The 6-Step chapters of this book are aimed at rectifying this lack of system and real confidence. They aim to create and sustain entrepreneurial flair. They end with action points that will help you build your business development plans for Asia as a whole, and for a number of individual Asian markets in particular, so that you can move ahead with patience but also with the requisite confidence.

It took me a while to build a reliable brand and reputation for my business. That was probably because I lacked the kind of long-term vision that this book encourages. It is easy to go into Asian markets with an ad hoc approach: a JV partner here, a supplier there, a referral, a government agency, a local representative, a subsidiary, an online affiliate, and many other such combinations. You may even think that you can do it more or less from your home city by videoconferencing backed up with a occasional visit, or by winging it with a bit of help from a local.

But there is no substitute for entering any of Asia's 21 or so markets (excluding the Indian subcontinent, which is a whole book by itself) with *personal understanding* and experience of the cultural attitudes and business practices that are prevalent, rather than simply relying on market or product research, suppliers and distributors and local partners.

Eventually I ended up as the speechwriter for a major multinational bank, writing speeches for the Chairman and CEO to give all over Asia and indeed all over the world as part of the preparations for Hong Kong's reversion to Chinese sovereignty in 1997. By the following year I had set up my own company, writing speeches and presentations for business and trade leaders and even politicians, first in Hong Kong and then in other Asian countries.

But it took me a long time to crack those other Asian markets. They didn't know me that well. They had cultural and business practices that were slightly different to those of Hong Kong. I had to learn other Asian business cultures and ways of doing things. Even though my previous work at the multinational bank had taken me to those countries, I was still a cultural novice in their eyes. I hadn't built the required long-term relationships or trust.

Every country in Asia is a challenge. That is another essential message of this book. Do not think you can automatically apply the knowledge gained about one Asian business culture (or culture as a whole) to another. If you have the skills and focus, if you have done the groundwork, if you have built the confidence through cultural understanding, you will probably be successful in more than one market. But to do that, you must also achieve mastery in more than one business culture.

So before we go any further, let's try to define what we mean by business culture. Because if you don't know what business culture is, and why it's so important, you will never be able to find the master key, let alone open the door.

Why is culture important in international business?

The cultural subtleties that influence international business reach far beyond the ability to greet your Asian counterpart correctly or choose an appropriate gift for a particular situation or present your business card in the right way.

The question of an individual culture's attitude to time and punctuality, whether the society is more collectivist in behaviour than individualist, the nuances of respect and hierarchy, not to mention body language and gestures and attitudes to 'harmony', can radically affect your understanding of the guy waiting in the next office or the woman across the dinner table, as well as your own chances of *being correctly understood*.

In a world of globalised business, the ubiquity of the internet and social media are no guarantee of avoiding unnecessary blunders (even insults!), while ignorance of who you are really dealing with may actively destroy your chances of building personal knowledge and creating the kind of credibility and trust that engenders long-term relationships and business success.

Even the way you frame your e-mails can jeopardise professional relationships across cultures. English may be a lingua franca, but in many countries of Asia this lingua franca conceals a strong attachment to local languages, customs, dialects and deep-rooted beliefs. Ignore them at your peril!

The key elements of Asian culture and business

As I have outlined, I have spent more than half my life working as a speechwriter and 'strategic messenger' for major multinationals and government institutions in the East, and the other half in the West. I have also written several books and given speeches and talks on Asian culture and business.

The knowledge I have gained has left me in no doubt that Asian culture can be influenced by economic activity. Anyone who has witnessed the rapid modernisation or South Korea or the impact of the markets on China in the last two decades will know that economics can indeed make a significant difference to cultural behaviour. However, this 'Westernizing' effect should not be exaggerated.

Despite the intrusion of market forces into much of the Chinese economy, the emphasis on relationships (*guanxi*) remains a core element of Chinese business culture. Connections are still paramount in much of Asia, taking precedence over money and markets even in cosmopolitan economies like Hong Kong and Singapore.

Cultural attitudes still influence other aspects of economic activity in Asia. Western standards of corporate governance, for example, do not necessarily sit well with the family-based, filial loyalty structure and ownership of many Asian corporations. Even in Hong Kong, conglomerates still make decisions with perhaps an octogenarian family patriarch as Chairman and a freshly installed forty-something MBA as CEO (although this situation is gradually changing).

Not all Asian companies view maximizing shareholder value as the core reason for their existence. Not all Asian financial models are based on economics alone. Islamic finance derives its business model from religious principles: the Koran's prohibition of earning interest from loans.

Asians identify more with the group and the family than with more individualistic behaviour. Confucianism, still deeply rooted in China, Hong Kong, Singapore, Taiwan and South Korea, teaches that respect for one's elders, the educated and those in authority forms the basis of society.

Buddhism, which had its roots in India, is based on a belief in reincarnation that is the result of karma in a previous life and on the accumulation of good deeds in order to achieve a better next life. The emphasis is on practise rather than worship of a higher god who intervenes in daily life, and on following the Middle Way rather than on attachment to material goods.

Taoism (and its variants throughout Southeast Asia and North Asia) also focuses on achieving a life of purity and simplicity, providing a comfort for ordinary people in turbulent times.

Finally, Asian culture has long been dominated by feudalism. For many centuries rich and privileged tyrants, warlords and government officers spread a culture of constant fear among ordinary, impoverished people throughout Asia. Even now, exaggerated respect and deference towards figures of authority and a reluctance to speak out are hallmarks of many Asian companies.

In line with this, more emphasis is still placed on the importance of family and relationships, of collective 'harmony' and authoritarian decision-making, rather than on individualism and the more frank and open discussion that marks Western decision-making.

Nevertheless, for Western businesses and entrepreneurs working in Asia, it is vital to recognize the strengths of the East that may not be so evident in their home countries. Once harnessed, these strengths can become positive assets in a company's business dealings and human resources departments.

To assist you in thinking about differences between Asian and Western business attitudes, I reproduce on the following page an excellent, if inevitably schematic comparison between Asian and Western thinking and behaviour from 'The Chinese Negotiation' by John L. Graham and N. Mark Lam, *Harvard Business Review*, October 2003.

	Asians	**Westerners**
Way of thinking		
Subject	holistic	individualistic
Social status	hierarchical	egalitarian
Relationship	beyond business	business networking
Logic	interrelated	sequential
Approach	authoritarian	open to discussion
Means	enforcement of order	fact-oriented
Channels	relationship	information
Duration	long-term	short- or medium-term

Business behaviour

Etiquette	formal	mostly informal
Meeting format	multiple objectives	clear objectives
Delegation	limited	authorized
Responsible party	normally unchanged	frequently changed
Information exchange	need-to-know basis	open exchange
Business proposal	arrived at indirectly	direct and open

Negotiation style	passive but persistent	direct and less patient
Priority setting	favourable total deal	principles and objectives
Expected partnership	long-term	business-driven

Action Points

1. Study the chart above and then put a ruler over each column in turn, both Asian and Western, to see if you can remember the difference in approach to each topic. You can practise this until you are more or less perfect. Thinking about the differences and what they might mean in real business terms will become second nature.

2. List out six cultural influences that you think are likely to make a difference in the way that Asian countries in general do business. Then map out the ways those influences (or some of them) may have an impact on the market or markets where you are operating or intend to operate.

3. Consider working with a coach or a local partner for the specific country market that you are targeting.

4. Get yourself informed about cultural differences by talking to local business people in the country itself. Expatriate 'old hands' are also worth consulting. This combination of preparatory coaching and local advice makes all the difference to whether you connect or not.

To make matters easier for you, I've designed an **'Asian Communication and Culture Cheat Sheet'**. All you need to do to access this special free bonus is to join my mailing list by following this link: http://davidcliveprice. com/the-master-key-to-asia-book-gift/

WHAT ARE THE BASICS OF ASIAN BUSINESS ETIQUETTE?

I READ SOMEWHERE RECENTLY that the best way to approach the differences of culture and etiquette in Asia between different countries, and to avoid confusion with Western cultural norms, is to group Asian countries under their primary means of eating: Chopsticks or Hands.

The Chopsticks countries include Japan, Korea, China, Hong, Kong, Taiwan, Singapore as well as the overseas Chinese in general. They are characterised by their governing 'Confucian' approach to doing business.

Hands countries, by contrast, include those largely Islamic peoples and nations that regard eating with the left hand as 'unclean' and therefore use the right hand to eat. These cultures include Malaysia, Indonesia, southern Thailand and Myanmar and are characterised by their adherence to deep spiritual beliefs.

The problem with such an arbitrary division of cultures is that it is both misleading and condescending. A proponent of the Chopsticks school of thought has written that the use of chopsticks in these countries reflects a 'non-rational' or 'illogical' cultural trait because eating with chopsticks is not the easiest, most hygienic or elegant way of consuming food. A proponent of the Hands school ventured that, although eating with the right hand suggested deep spiritual beliefs, it was also an uncomfortable and irrational habit.

Neither Western commentator thought fit to point out that chopsticks were the logical answer to eating from a rice bowl and transferring delicate pieces of food to that bowl from communal dishes in the centre of the table. Nor did they remark that the Koran places a special emphasis on community and family, hence communal eating that allows for food to be wrapped in breads.

Quite apart from the cultural ignorance such generalisations reflect, such arbitrary divisions confuse more than they inform. It is true that various Asian countries often have different cultures with aspects of etiquette that are uniquely theirs. But as a general rule, it is true to say that almost all Asian cultures have more deep-seated and widespread spiritual beliefs than Western ones. In terms of business etiquette, this often translates into a higher degree of formality, more gestures of respect, and more concern with correct titles, among other refined manners.

Such questions go to the heart of this book. For what differentiates almost all Western business people that are successful in Asia, as well as almost all successful business travellers, is that they have learned to see the culture of the country they in which they are a visitor *from another viewpoint* to their own, more Western-oriented culture.

They are able to enter into the spirit of that country through willingness, preparation, emotional intelligence, empathy and lateral thinking. To take a simple example, ask yourself whether you would be flattered to be called 'primitive hunter-gatherers' because you still eat with a knife and fork. Or whether you would be happy to be termed 'inelegant' because you were hooked on McDonald's burgers (which you eat with your hands, by the way).

These are not incidental questions. Countless surveys have concluded that the way you present yourself in the office and work environment accounts for almost 80 per cent of business success. Business is often based on first and on-going impressions, body language, common courtesies and attention to small details. How much truer is this in an Asian context, where fitting in and collective 'harmony' are at a premium, as well as building long-lasting relationships and saving face (avoiding embarrassment) at all costs.

The role of women

Western businesswomen have a distinct advantage over men in this regard. It is a commonly held belief in Western countries that gender equality has a poor record in Asian cultures. Businesswomen are supposedly given far less respect and attention then in many Western countries.

Confucianism dictates that women are subservient to and should always obey 'father, husband and son'. In the stricter forms of Islam, similar beliefs are held in regard to women's place and role in family and society. Women in some Asian countries have long been held back by the lack of professional, political and educational opportunities on offer to men.

However, these attitudes are rapidly changing (South Korea has recently elected its first woman president). Even though women's presence is still rare in some Asian business circles, women are rapidly moving into leadership positions elsewhere. It is worth noting that almost 50 per cent of the senior executives in China are women, and that in Asia as a whole 29 per cent of the senior executive positions are held by women as compared to 24 per cent in Europe. Don't assume that the Asian woman in the room is a junior manager about to pour the tea.

Asians do direct some resistance to women in business but this is mainly at local women, not at Westerners. This is possibly because Asians have begun to see women, at least those from outside their own society, as equal to men because of their emotional intelligence. Women are increasingly perceived as smart negotiators, softly spoken and persuasive, good at instinctive reactions and listening, more able than men to seek out common ground and explore client's needs, more patient and curious about other people and their lifestyles.

In other words, Western women have an increased chance of business success in many Asian countries (not all) because they rely more on the 'feel' and 'context' of a business situation, rather than on immediate gains and direct outcomes.

In countries like Japan and Korea, where business is still highly male-dominated, women executives will have to pay extra attention to demonstrating their seniority through the local etiquette protocols (see Step Four). But Western businesswomen whose behaviour accords with Asian male preconceptions can be and often are readily accepted.

General etiquette rules across Asia

Asian countries are considered to be 'high context' cultures. In a high context culture many things are left unsaid, letting the culture do the explaining. Asians believe they must know and trust someone before they are willing to enter into a business agreement or make a business decision. Depending on the particular economy and how deeply it is influenced by Western models, communication is largely indirect and reliant on tone of voice, gestures, behaviour at formal occasions and respect systems.

A straightforward 'yes' or 'no' is not usually offered to a direct question, especially in a country like Japan. On the other hand, Asians are often persistent, if passive negotiators.

Westerners largely come from 'low context' cultures. They communicate directly, get to the point and move on quickly in business so as not to 'waste time', even if they don't know someone well. Action and getting down to business are viewed as priorities, which often means that 'high context' Asians view their Western counterparts as impatient, insincere or casual. Or all three together!

Of course there is nothing wrong with getting to the point in business negotiations. However, in Asia it is generally considered more appropriate to take these negotiations step by step, drawing in and referring to each person or department responsible for each aspect of the deal. When all parties are fully convinced that their concerns are covered, the trust is built that ensures a long-term relationship.

For those who are unwilling or unable to spend sufficient time in Asia to achieve this, a parachute in-and-out visit will not be of much assistance. It is vital that your company's local representative maintains ongoing contact and interaction with your proposed partner, and that trust is developed to the extent that your Asian partner or client is assured of the total value of the deal in the long term. For Asian businessmen, this is far preferable to short-term business deals that always have to begin again from scratch when the next step is negotiated (the Western 'economics-trumps-relationships' approach).

Here are some of the more obvious business etiquette tips that are generally applicable to all countries across Asia. More detailed country-specific guides are provided in Step Three.

Business attire

As a general rule, play safe and be conservative with suits, ties and tie-up shoes for men, and unrevealing semi-formal suits and dresses for women. A business meeting, lunch or dinner or even drinking coffee together tend to be rather formal, at least at the outset, with handshakes, exchange of business cards, discreet inspections and elaborate courtesies about who is paying (usually the host), and so on.

In warmer climates, a smart shirt and tie and slacks or even an open-necked shirt may be permissible, but check what business people are wearing before you make your choice. A suit may be still be preferred in tropical, heavily air-conditioned Hong Kong or during summer in

Japan and Korea, depending on the industry and sector. The most relaxed garb is found in Vietnam, Malaysia and the Philippines, but even in these countries avoid anything flashy or ultra-fashionable.

Personal branding

Many Western business people going into Asia forget that one of the most essential ways to open doors and forge lasting business relationships is personal branding. That may sound strange, as if you have to become a Richard Branson or Steve Jobs to succeed. But it's amazing how many people fall down when it comes to projecting themselves and their company.

Part of the challenge is clear communication: how to speak clearly and at a regular pace in a foreign culture without complicating your language. You have to make sure you're understood. But there's more to it than that. Personal branding goes to the heart of what you are trying to sell or promote: You!

If you are walk though almost any Asian capital from Seoul to Beijing, from Tokyo to Singapore, from Hong Kong to Kuala Lumpur, you will be knocked out by the sheer amount of visual stimulus: stylish architecture, huge billboards with beautiful actors or actresses and singers, models, top-of-the-line cars, world-class cosmetics and fashion.

The various countries of Asia have youthful and dynamic cultures. The younger generation often form a majority of their populations. Their idols fill the airwaves and the TV channels. Everywhere, stylishness and modernity are on display. Therefore, those who desire success in the marketplaces of Asia should sit up and take notice.

A major element of the Asian emphasis on 'context' for assessing business partners is *what you look like*. That may sound superficial but it's true. The visual first impression you give in what are increasingly smart, sophisticated, cosmopolitan and cultured Asian business circles is what really counts.

Your face, your clothing, your body language and your speech are all part of what an Asian counterpart will conclude about you. This may sound like the Hollywood hang-up on image. It may strike you as nothing to do with someone who is selling widgets in Chongqing.

But in Asia the visual goes beyond simply image. The good (well educated, professional) impression you make is often the entry point for further conclusions about you, such as your truthfulness, diligence, kindness, intelligence and loyalty. These values will form part of the impression a Korean or a Japanese, a Malaysian or a Chinese makes as to whether they can work with you. They will contribute to the 'feeling' that an Asian has about you. In almost every Asian country, this unspoken 'feeling' is what cements the relationship. The image you project of stylishness will see you categorized into boxes labelled 'social class', 'education', 'potential' and '*I want to be seen with you*'.

So if you are entering Asia markets for the first time, or want to up your game in Asia, just remember that if you ask an Asian's opinion about a friend or a politician or a potential employee, they will often say 'They *look* like a good or clever or trustworthy' person.'

The good news is that this emphasis is on appearance doesn't mean that you have to undergo cosmetic surgery in Korea, Japan or the Philippines! You just have to take care with your personal presentation. Go to the gym and lose some pounds, sort out your wardrobe, get well scrubbed and regularly mosturized, drop the biro and invest in a Mont Blanc, buy a good watch and put away the Swatch. Each of these details will be quickly assessed and noted as part of your personal branding. Each of them will mark you out as being 'worth it'.

No one has ever been looked down upon for dressing up a bit or dressing slightly more conservatively. In Asia, a 'low level person' is unshaven or wearing a check shirt and baggy chinos or a revealing beach-type dress at a business meeting. If you want to gain millionaire status in Asia, you have to be on the money. You have to 'get the rules'. And the number one rule is good personal branding.

Punctuality

It is a sign of respect all over Asia to be on time for appointments. This is particularly true in Japan, but even in less clockwork societies like China and Hong Kong, being late is considered rude. If the traffic is bad, as it is bound to be in countries like Thailand, the Philippines and even South Korea, don't over-schedule and always call ahead if late. This saves your face (it is your hosts' country and their traffic problems) and also that of your local partner.

As a general rule, arrive early and find what Americans aptly call the 'comfort room'. It is very uncomfortable to sit through meetings with a full bladder after a long delay in traffic.

The language barrier

In many Asian countries, English is reasonably or well spoken as a second language (first language in Singapore). However, in countries such as Japan, Korea and China, this might not always be the case. In particular, English is less spoken outside the main cities of these countries and the signage is almost entirely in local script with no English translation in sight.

You should assess the likelihood of communication difficulties beforehand, particularly if highly technical matters are involved, and appoint a trustworthy and recommended interpreter such as the local marketing officers attached to home country embassies or consulates.

It is best to discuss the necessity for an interpreter with your local contacts, such as your local partner, agent or distributor, who may well be able to act as interpreters and guides themselves if required. They will also help you avoid giving offence by taking an interpreter along to a meeting when the Asian party speaks and understands English well. Key selection criteria for an agent or partner should include their ability to communicate and manage relationships across the East-West cultural divide. It is vital to take time to find the right partner.

Visitors to Asian trade fairs should avoid hiring interpreters that offer their services at the gates of the fair. They are not dependable. It is better to find one beforehand from the recommended list of the trade fair website or by word of mouth from a trusted source within the country, such as a local agent, distributor or expat 'old hand'.

Correct manner of address

When addressing someone, always err on the conservative side. Don't assume that you can use the informal first name as Westerners often do. Go with the more formal title of Mr. or Mrs. or even Dr. if appropriate (Asians tend to be very respectful about education and qualifications). Also, remember that married women always retain their maiden name.

In Japan, it's slightly more complicated since it's usual to add an honorific to the last name of a client (for a man this would be '-san' as in 'Watanabe-san') instead of using 'Mr.' However, it is not appropriate to use the honorific when referring to your colleague or a family member, since that puts them higher on the respect scale than a Japanese person would consider appropriate.

Chinese surnames are usually first in what is usually a three-name series: Li ka-shing. But when introducing guests, they usually use full titles and company names, such as Doctor Michael Williams, CEO of United International Bank. You should do the same for the Chinese.

The Thais replace Mr. with 'Khun', the Filipinos will often call you 'Sir' or 'Madam' before your Christian name (if you are known and trusted) or before your surname. The South Koreans use both their full three-part name like the Chinese, and also a shortened Western form (Mr. Park and Miss Kim). The Myanmarese usually use their entire name with various honorifics (Ma Ma Naing or U Khin Nyunt) and they would expect you to do the same.

In other words, the overall rule is simple: don't shorten anyone's name or create a nickname for them. If they really like and trust you, and you are not very senior management, you may end up being called 'Mr. David' or 'Sir David' or 'Khun David' or even 'David' as I have been in various Asian countries.

But don't assume that will be the case. It depends on the length of the relationship, the level of your acceptance and your seniority. It also depends on how Westernized is the prevailing culture. The Hong Kong or Singaporean Chinese may refer to you by your Christian name, but only after the relationship is established and you have begun to do business together.

Handshake or bow?

At the initial and indeed at all consequent meetings with your Asian counterparts, watch out for the Mr. Bean moment. By that I mean being put off by the formal bows, or clasping of the hands to the forehead, or other gestures of respect and greeting that your hosts may adopt with each other and occasionally with you. Do not be tempted.

I have had some hilarious moments in the foyers of Thai or Korean luxury hotels or fancy Japanese receptions when in my formal suit I have attempted to replace or follow the usual Western handshake with a more Eastern bow or tenting of the hands to the forehead.

Sometimes my imitative gestures would work. Usually, I ended up looking like Mr. Bean about to keel over.

The general rule is: stick to the handshake. It is a quite common greeting when doing business in Asia (although Muslim women will not shake hands with men). When a hand is proffered, shake it immediately, but again not in a Mr. Bean way by pumping it or holding on too long or too firmly. Filipinos are especially open to handshakes and are generally more Americanized and relaxed about etiquette.

Both the Japanese and the Koreans have been called 'the great ceremonious people of the East', and bowing between business colleagues (and almost anyone of equal or higher standing) is an accepted sign of respect. But unless you have been coached, or have been living in Asia a long while, it is better to go for the handshake.

If you feel confident, a slight bow of the head can accompany the handshake. In China, a group may greet you or your group with applause: simply applaud back. A slight concession to Eastern traditions is often the key to successful business relations in Asia.

In general, Asians are understated. They do not appreciate body contact with strangers such as back slapping or touching, clicking fingers, pointing with index fingers (use an open hand facing downwards), whistling, legs on the table, placing your feet in the vicinity of someone's head, leaving hands in pockets or sucking in air loudly to express surprise.

Presenting your business card

This is a subject that creates a minefield of misunderstandings. However, there is no reason why this should be so. Presenting your credentials is an obvious way of initiating business contact in both East and West. Business people all over the world send out individual and company portfolios and resumés, create websites and use social media such as Facebook and LinkedIn, to initiate business.

The only major difference is that Westerners tend to be more relaxed about introducing themselves, or at least less formal, and do not use business cards much. Even when they do, the cards are often handed out in a cocktail party way with one hand on a glass of something and the other flicking the card into a convenient side pocket.

Asia is very different in this regard. It is generally considered that a business card represents a person's identity. The card is literally the *face* of you and your business: who you are and what position you hold. Just as we wouldn't mistreat a face by scribbling on it, or by offering it with a flick of the hand, or by dumping it into a back pocket wallet to be sat on, so too the Asian business card demands respect.

There is a rite that follows on a first meeting, just after the handshake and initial exchange of names. That is the exchange of business cards. And just as in any rite, there are simple rules to observe.

First, make sure that the business card has all your details and is printed in English on one side and the local language on the other. If the language is Chinese, the characters should be simplified Chinese for mainland China and Singapore, traditional for Hong Kong/Taiwan.

The Japanese call business cards *meishi*, and *meishi* have much greater cultural significance in Japan than in Western culture. They provide information about the group to which you belong, where you stand in the respect hierarchy rather and therefore how much respect should be shown to you. Not presenting a *meishi* at a business meeting is tantamount to not shaking hands a Western business meeting. It causes irreparable damage.

Second, always stand up to exchange cards. The cards themselves should be meticulously clean and if possible produced from an elegant cardholder. Bent or smudged or worn-out cards will not do. Present your card with both thumbs holding the card in front of you, NOT in one hand as if your are about to play poker. The local language should be on the upper side of the card. If required (and it usually is, since everyone at the meeting will come armed with their own cards), continue to present your cards one-by-one, individual-by-individual, using both hands if possible. Remember you have to accept the other person's business card in the same respectful manner, so if you are new to the game, practise with your colleagues until you get the rhythm and the presentation fluent.

Third, observe some simple 'dos' and 'don'ts'. Don't toss the cards about in any manner. Don't place a stack of them on the table and ask people to help themselves. Don't put the card away in an inner pocket, or worse, lose it somewhere in your trousers or skirt pockets. Leave it out with the others on the tabletop as the meeting proceeds so that you can refer to it (your Asian counterparts will find this respectful and take note).

Don't write comments on anyone else's business card in their presence, such as when the client is available, next meeting, mobile number etc., since this is equivalent to writing on their face. Many Asian clients hand out their business cards as if there were no tomorrow. Don't be left out. Take an ample supply of cards with you to every meeting. You will use many more of them than in your home country.

Saving face

In general, Asians are extremely sensitive about face: losing face, saving face or giving face to another person. The Japanese are extremely reluctant to say 'no', or even conceded that there is a problem, and will usually give an impenetrable answer to a straight question in order to hide their real thought or meaning. Filipinos may reluctantly agree to something, only to forget all about it when you are conveniently off the scene. Thais hide their horror of confrontation behind smiles. Bahasa Indonesian, the language of Indonesia, has twelve ways to say 'no'.

This obliqueness is very hard for 'individualist' Westerners to understand, but it stems from the unwillingness to upset the collective harmony. Obliqueness and respect for harmony are hallmarks of Asian cultures. Contradicting someone openly, criticising them in front of someone else, putting them in awkward situations or patronising them are a sure way to lose business. They make it impossible to save face. Always *give* face through sincere compliments, showing respect or doing something that raises self-esteem.

How to be wined and dined

As I have said, if you are planning to do business in Asia, it is essential to remember that the Asian approach is not necessarily direct and 'let's get down to business', especially when meeting socially (for example, for dinner). Most Asian cultures expect the approach to be indirect, even circuitous, and above all based on getting to know the Western counterpart in order to build a relationship of trust, credibility and human empathy.

Since Asia cultures are so family-oriented, this often means that enquiries and discussion about family and social background/circumstances, home and hobbies, initially take precedence over direct business negotiations. At a first business meeting, especially a formal lunch or dinner (a banquet of at least eight courses in Hong Kong and China), business is often not expected to be the primary topic. Asian business partners want to get to know you, not your bottom line. They want to know if there is likely to be longevity in the relationship, if they can get on with you, if you have the ability to work in harmony with their business and social culture.

Here are some basic tips for those essential dinner meetings:

- Be on time

- Exchange business cards, holding the card as a rectangle in front of you to present as instructed above

- Expect to be slightly formal to begin with, exchange handshakes if offered, don't bow even if bowed to

- Let the host order

- Don't talk business

- Try everything put before you (you don't have to finish it, just pick).

- Dishes might includes sushi or sashimi in Japan, a wide variety of unusual animal delicacies in China, fiery kimchi (chilli and cabbage) in Korea, various gradations of Thai curry, and more or less anything in Hong Kong

- Be prepared not to turn your nose up but instead offer the local word for delicious (*ho-may* or *ho-sek* in Hong Kong and China, *sarap* in the Philippines, *oy-ishi* in Japan etc.). Leaving some food is a compliment, suggesting the meal is too good to finish

- Be concerned about your host's family, friends, daily life, and so on

- Have a few words of the local language (even 'thank you' or 'yes' and 'no' gets you a long way in the business relations stakes)

- Be polite to the waiters, even if they're not polite to you or don't conform to your standards

- Be complimentary (for example, about the local transport, culture, temple you've seen, city's modernity, local food etc)

- Toast only after the host toasts, but accept any toast in your direction with a sip of your wine and a slightly raised glass.

- Don't get drunk, even if they do: a doctor's advice to be moderate is an easily accepted excuse. Sip slowly, because your beer glass or wine cup will be immediately refilled

- If tea is involved, the locals will also regularly refill your cup. Acknowledge the refills with two fingers bent downwards on the table top

- Let the host pay

In China and Hong Kong, entertaining usually takes place at a well-known bar or restaurant. Similarly, in Japan, your host will take you out to wine and dine for a whole evening (sometimes with karaoke, be warned). Koreans, however, like to entertain both in restaurants and at home.

If you're going to a private home, arrive on time and bring a small but delicate gift (for suitable gifts for individual countries, see Step Four). Most Korean homes, as with many homes in China, Hong Kong, Vietnam, Singapore, Malaysia, Indonesia, the Philippines and Japan, have a small lobby or cupboard where outdoor shoes are to be left and slippers put on. Don't walk straight onto the clean floor!

Drinking and karaoke

In some Asian cultures, relationship building may well be dependent on the amount of alcohol consumed during evening 'entertainment' sessions. This is particularly true in China, Japan and Korea. Since some of the local drinks, such as Chinese rice wine, Japanese saké and Korean soju, can be up to 50 per cent or more proof, it is best to be extremely careful about getting drunk (sipping beer or giving a medical reason for drinking soft drinks are acceptable alternatives).

Don't comment or even feign surprise if your counterpart becomes drunk, and don't mention it the next day. Not all Asians approve of drinking alcohol. Devout Muslims and some devout Buddhists don't drink it and you shouldn't if your Asian colleagues abstain. In particular, women should abstain in public places if the local culture disapproves.

Evening drinking is some Asian countries is invariably followed or accompanied by karaoke sessions or visits to karaoke bars. Visiting Westerners should expect to take part in these as an integral part of relationship building particularly in China, Japan and Korea. My solution is to prepare in advance a small repertoire of two or three numbers that you can repeat everywhere. I have lost count of the number of times I have rolled out 'New York, New York' or 'Don't Cry for Me Argentina' in Hong Kong, Seoul, Tokyo, Beijing and Manila. My renditions didn't improve, but the relationships did.

Action Points

1. If you are not entirely clear what is meant by a low context and high context culture, go back over this chapter and list out some of the major differences in business approach between your customary business circles and what you may encounter in Asian business circles.

2. Consider how you might improve your personal branding to make a good impression on your Asian partners. What practical steps can you take to raise your game?

3. Think of an occasion on which you might have prevented your Asian counterpart from losing face, or yourself from losing face, and consider how you might have done things differently to avoid any suggestion of offence or negatively impacting a business negotiation.

4. Go back over the Asian business etiquette tips and practice with a colleague how they might be applied in action: for example, the exchange of business cards, introducing yourself and addressing your counterpart, accepting a toast at a business meal, and so on.

5. Actively seek advice on local business customs, etiquette and mistakes to avoid from your local partner or members of your local team. This learning process takes time, effort and sensitivity.

ARE ASIAN VALUES A MYTH OR A REALITY?

Culture and ethics in Asian business

There is a common myth among Westerners that all Asian countries share the same 'Asian values', attitudes and approach to business. In past decades Asian politicians like Lee Kuan Yew, the father of Singapore, or Dr. Mahathir of Malaysia have supported this myth by drawing attention to the 'decadence' of Western individualism and by declaring that the economic strength of their countries is due to a strong collectivist culture based on Confucian values such as order, respect, hierarchy and harmony.

'Too much democracy' is cited as the reason for social instability in the West, freedom of speech as the generator of cultural weakness, unfettered individualism as the cause of the breakdown of group and family consciousness. These stereotypes have taken root in the way that Westerners think about Asian business and culture. To a certain extent they have some basis in reality but they are by no means the whole truth. They obscure significant differences of culture between, say, China, Japan, Thailand and the Philippines.

It is true that participatory democracy is relatively subdued or absent in many countries in Asia. It is also true that the emphasis on group and family collectivism, authority and hierarchy, respect and paternalism have led to serious distortions of business ethics in some Asian countries such as the encouragement of crony capitalism, favoured treatment for financial loans and family nepotism.

But whether corruption is more an Asian trait or a Western one is debatable. The revelations since 2008 of what has transpired in the financial markets of the West suggest that the more individualist West's tendency to allow workers greater freedom to operate on their own has encouraged a widespread culture of insider trading, manipulation of markets and inter-bank collusion.

Whatever their relative merits or drawbacks, Asian values have proved extremely beneficial for building the foundations of a country's prosperity, especially when competent economists and technocrats (many of them educated in the West) are allowed to guide team-conscious and highly trained people. Asian values could be said to have fostered high savings rates and hence substantial capital for economic growth. The average savings rate in China is around 50 per cent as a percentage of income, one of the highest in the world.

The Asian passion for education has produced an almost unlimited supply of educated labour and high-quality engineers. In addition, the stricter regimes imposed by society and schools, as well as compulsory military service in many countries, have produced disciplined workers that respond well to clearly defined routines and working in a team.

Western business executives working in Asia would do well to recognize the strengths of the Asian model and to consider how it could become the backbone for economic success in their own countries.

Work Ethic

It is easy to forget that many of the glittering Asian economies that we see today have in fact become successful only in relatively recent times. Even though China's 'socialist market economy' became the second largest economy in the world in 2010, the market-oriented reforms that were instigated by Deng xiao-ping only really took off in the 1990s. Given such rapid progress, it is perhaps no surprise that China has still not managed to close the enormous gap between the privileged few and the vast majority of the population.

Similarly, the Asian Tiger economies of Hong Kong, Singapore, Taiwan, South Korea, Malaysia and Thailand grew substantially between the late 1980s and early- to mid-1990s with the injection of large amounts of foreign investment capital. They then experienced a financial crisis in 1997-98 due to huge debt-servicing expenses and (again) an inequitable distribution of wealth, since most of the wealth remained in the control of an élite few. Since the late 1990s, these economies have recovered well and have become increasingly active participants in the global market. In more recent times, they have been joined by the Philippines, Vietnam and Indonesia.

However, most Asia Tiger economies, including Hong Kong and Singapore, still have a long way to go to close the wealth gap. In addition, many of these countries have experienced the birth pangs of nationhood, political upheaval or post-conflict reconstruction from the 1960s onwards. It is little wonder that their work ethic is the envy of the world.

Even now, when you might expect Asians to take their foot off the accelerator, Asians continue to work as if they were still poor. It has been estimated that the average Singaporean works 2,307 hours a year and the average Hong Konger 2,287 hours per year, whereas the average European works 1,625 hours a year with four week's holiday. This means that a Singaporean is working the equivalent of four months a year more than an average European. For anyone attempting to do business in Asia, it is important to take into account this high and relentless work ethic.

Family ownership

The downside of Asian values derives from the attitude that the interests of family and close friends must be protected at all costs and placed before the public interest. 'Family' can be interpreted to include the inner circle or loyal subordinate or even government officers. The relationship of trust that these 'family' members have developed means that major transactions are sometimes executed without legal due diligence and the usual commercial procedures.

This tradition derives from the 'gentlemen's agreements' prevalent in Asian business circles in the past and that still characterize the approach to contracts and decisions in several Asian countries today. Although some deference is paid to legal and corporate governance requirements, the overwhelming factor determining the outcome of business negotiations in Asia is usually trust and the length of the relationship. It is therefore essential to have a clear understanding of the nuances of Asian social and business culture before entering into negotiations with an Asian partner or beginning business operations in Asia.

One of the most pervasive aspects of Asian business cultures is the determination of founding families to retain control. The contrast with Western business cultures based on the Anglo-Saxon model, where shareholder value is paramount, is marked.

The function of the firm in the private sector in China, for example, is primarily to generate family wealth. Most of China's new class of millionaires come from profitable family-owned businesses. The firms exist to provide shareholder value only for people at the very top, which is why many large Chinese companies are governed more hierarchically than their Western counterparts.

In Japan, by contrast, the purpose of the Japanese firm is not solely to maximize shareholder value but to adopt a more family-like focus and strive to take care of their employees (although lifetime employment is now long gone). The firm is the family. In Taiwan, the Chinese family still has a strong influence on how businesses are organized and expanded, even more so under the impact of globalization.

Such patronage systems reinforce feelings of mutual dependency, obligation, loyalty and trust. 'Gifts' made by a patron are unstated and not immediately reciprocated but such favours can be called in at a later date. A patronage relationship can last a lifetime.

Personal connections are therefore vital to getting things done.

Corporate governance

Among the reasons that family businesses in Asia seek to retain control is that costs of internal auditing and reporting are thereby lowered, succession issues and compensation systems are more comfortably handled, and publicly listed companies can be treated as personal fiefdoms. Although much stronger corporate governance regimes have been established in international financial centres with developed capital markets such as Hong Kong and Singapore, it is true that a widening gap remains between laws and implementation in many Asian countries.

A more dynamic regulatory environment, together with the increasing complexity of business transactions and significant advances in information technology, has resulted in an upgrade of the corporate governance framework in various Asian countries. However, corporate social responsibility (CSR) and protection of the environment do not feature strongly in the corporate reputation agenda of many Asian executives. In Hong Kong, the CSR chapters of annual reports have become steadily larger but performance and implementation remain patchy.

A recent survey of six Chinese cities found that environmental awareness was strong amongst managers and local government officials but implementation was hampered by the fear of sacrificing economic growth. I recently interviewed the Chairman of a family-owned

Chinese firm who said he knew nothing of environmental matters ('I leave that to HR') and very little about CSR issues. However, as Chairman and CEO combined, he was aware of succession issues and was considering splitting the roles 'at a future date'.

Corruption

Corruption exists in all societies, not least in the financial markets of the West. In Asia, patronage systems and collectivism have inevitably encouraged corruption in one form of another, which has flourished according to the relative strength or weakness of the rule of law.

In Japan, Singapore, Hong Kong and Taiwan, corruption is limited due to robust regulatory systems and the rule of law. In Thailand or the Philippines, bloated government bureaucracies have ensured that 'gifts' to obtain almost any permit or gesture of cooperation are part of a common culture.

In China, although legal protection is weaker, one of the most effective anti-corruption factors for private sector firms is the sharing of prospective high profits. This prospect aligns the interests of government officials with those of entrepreneurs and investors, thereby ensuring that all parties fulfil their roles and protect the firm's reputation to make the enterprise successful.

Generally speaking, Asian executives rate corruption well below inflation and inadequate infrastructure or labour regulations as an obstacle to doing business. In part this is because Western law has not been central to Asian experience except in countries like Hong Kong and Singapore that were under colonial rule for a long time.

Singapore prides itself on being a meritocracy with a bureaucracy that is transparent and limited, and where people are aware of the rules and play by them. Hong Kong is rather Westernized with a legal system, civil service and police force that were purged of official corruption over the last forty years by a corruption monitoring body called the Independent Commission Against Corruption (ICAC).

China, by contrast is said not to have rule of law, but rule *by* law. A successful entrepreneur or a government official will command a large project to be done and it will be done. His power may be theoretically limited by the need for permits, but he will order his lawyers to find a law that allows what he wants, or he will even get a new law passed. Anyone who wants to do business in Asia should be aware of the variety of legal systems in operation, and of their relative strengths and weaknesses.

Drivers of consumer behaviour

If there is any difference in the pursuit of quality of life between East and West, it lies in the obsessive determination of Asian people to achieve success along with all the visible trappings of that success. In addition to saving money for their children's education (the best that can be bought), they strive to buy an apartment or house, a prestigious car or two, an overseas family holiday, as well as brand name bags, jewellery, watches, clothes and electronic goods that reflect their social status.

High savings rates in countries like Japan, China, Singapore, Hong Kong and Taiwan help them in their quest to lead a better life for themselves, and for the family as a whole to prosper.

Most Asians regard a higher educational degree as one of the most important drivers of economic and social success. Even before their children are born, they are being allocated schools and budgets and possible university places. This devotion to education derives from family ambition, competition, tradition and culture as well as a deep-rooted respect for knowledge and expertise. Education leads to social recognition, which is a major priority in Asian life. The number and quality of brand name products owned by any single individual is further testimony to this need for social recognition.

Much the same can be said of luxury consumers in Western countries, except that Asians seem to pursue their materialist goals with a passion that expresses itself in highly visible ways. Luxury brands such as Gucci, Louis Vuitton, Chanel, Mercedes-Benz, BMW, Rolex, Cartier, all are at the top of Asian consumers' shopping lists, along with Cuban cigars, membership of private clubs, hotel and airline rewards programmes, and the latest Apple or Samsung phones or laptops.

As the Asian economies continue to outperform those in the rest of the world, these high-end consumer markets will further grow and mature. According to the Brookings Institution, by 2015 the number of Asian middle class consumers will equal the number in Europe and North America. By 2021, on present trends, there could be more than 2 billion Asians in middle class households. In China alone, there could be over 670 million middle class consumers (almost half the population), compared with only perhaps 150 million today.

Western businesses cannot afford to be left behind. They must fully educate themselves on the beliefs, habits, traditions, background and tastes of these Asian consumers, learn how to interact and communicate with them, tailor their products and brands accordingly and be ready to build long-term relationships in the countries where they live.

Action Points

1. List out the Asian values you most admire and consider whether they are equally to be found in Western countries. For example, could they become the backbone of economic success in your own country or are they already in operation there in some form? If so, what makes these values so successful in Asia while your own more 'developed' country seems to be lagging behind?

2. Consider where regulatory systems, the rule of law and corporate governance regimes are strongest in Asia, and how this may or may not affect your business strategies.

3. Name what you regard as the top drivers of Asian consumer and social behaviour, and ask yourself whether these trends play a significant part of your business expansion plans.

4. Actively seek out and take advice from experienced expats and local Thais, Vietnamese, Chinese, and

so on in the market or markets you choose, so that your are fully prepared for market entry and development.

5. Make sure you choose highly intelligent, well educated and strongly motivated local partners and members of your local team. Take advice from them on all cultural, political and social matters that may impact your business.

STEP FOUR

BUSINESS CULTURE IN ASIAN COUNTRIES – WHAT SHOULD I REALLY KNOW?

As mentioned in Step One, it does not automatically follow that business success and cultural confidence in one Asian culture will translate to success in another, however much they may seem to be related. Personally, I struggled for years to establish my own brand and business outside Hong Kong and even now the progress I have made is not equal in every market I have tried to penetrate.

Asia is a 'patchwork quilt' of economic models, national characteristics, cultures, languages, beliefs, customs and etiquettes. Although this chapter provides a country-by-country guide to some of the most significant characteristics, they are not intended to impose stereotypes or be in any way definitive.

Most Asian countries share beliefs and customs in common. However, there are often important gradations from country to country, just as there are subtle differences within those countries based on ethnic and religious groups, shared history, geographical area, the assumptions of business, corporate and political élites, and so on.

There can be no one-size-fits-all approach to Asian cultures and etiquettes, not even within one country. It would also be ridiculous to assume that the cultural and national traits identified in this chapter apply to every single individual from that country. There may be Japanese or Korean business people that are far more demonstrative and casual than this chapter suggests, or Filipinos or Indonesians that are far more reserved and formal. However, the attempt to make sense of the cultural and business environment of individual Asia countries is undoubtedly an essential step towards building a successful business.

The country guides that follow are an attempt to provide a better understanding of Asian business practices and cultures while helping you avoid unnecessary embarrassment or giving offence. They are stepping-stones into worlds that will require much more detailed attention as your business develops.

Since some of the cultures are closely related or overlapping, especially those in which the Chinese are a majority, some sections such as those on Chinese New Year or gift giving, dining out or presenting business cards are inevitably similar. This chapter is more a reference manual for researching those countries or cultures in which you have a particular interest, rather than a chapter to be read through in its entirety.

Once you have absorbed the introduction to the country in which you have a special interest, it will be time to go deeper into those aspects that will particularly impact and promote your business for the long term.

The developed economies – Hong Kong, Taiwan, Singapore, Japan, South Korea

Hong Kong

Hong Kong is one of the most cosmopolitan cities in Asia. Nowadays it is also increasingly Chinese. Since the return of Hong Kong to China in 1997 when Britain's lease on Kowloon ended, both the general culture and business culture are becoming gradually more integrated with those of Mainland, and both sides of the border are trying to assimilate the other's best practices.

However, business efficiency, the rule of law, obsessive hard work (until all hours) and consciousness of the city's role as a bridge to the Mainland way of doing things, have all remained from the colonial era. The legal system, the civil service and the police are all relatively free of corruption, factors that together with the city's excellent infrastructure attract foreign businesses from all over the world to set up headquarters or regional offices.

Hong Kong is one of the region's premier trading hubs, vital in the supply chain for Chinese goods, and a business centre where the lack of red tape, low tax environment, and sheer efficiency provide an ideal environment for fund-raising and doing deals. Despite the local population being 95 per cent Chinese, most of them speaking the local dialect of Cantonese, English is still the lingua franca of business transactions, financial reporting and services. Many young people and shop service personnel speak at least some English, although the standard is gradually declining in preference for Mandarin (spoken by the many Mainland tourists and in government circles).

Buddhism and Confucianism are the predominant local beliefs. Confucian respect for seniority and authority sits well with the large number of Hong Kong family businesses with their extended networks and controlling styles. Unlike multinationals, these businesses give little freedom or discretion to their employees and are not multicultural but heavily dependent on ethnic Chinese. Those businesses backed by Chinese capital tend be less efficient and flexible in allocating resources, with less transparency and weaker governance (although this trend is gradually changing).

Confucianism and the family

As in most Asian societies, the family plays an important role in Hong Kong. This focus on the family derives partly from age-old Confucian beliefs (there are many Confucian schools in the city), which emphasise the duties of people to one another based on the closeness of their relationship. Filial piety, respect for age, loyalty and sincerity are the hallmarks of Confucianism and are reflected in the respect for hierarchies in both families and business.

Not that Hong Kong Chinese are overly formal. They have a strong sense of humour and are fun loving, but only in the right context. The boss is all, and so are the bosses under him (or sometimes her). A foreigner attending a business meeting in Hong Kong may be misled into thinking the environment is Western casual (apart from the business attire). But do not be deceived.

Not only is there an obvious pecking order about who sits where and who talks when, but there is also a subtle deference system in action that it is best for the outsider to observe and follow.

Meeting and greeting

Most of these rules are fairly simple. The Hong Kong Chinese shake hands rather than bowing but in a delicate way, without the Texan enthusiasm of a George Bush Jr. They don't tend to stare you straight in the eye and they won't expect you to obviously analyse or eyeball them during the meeting. If it's a large reception you may have to introduce yourself to the other guests but at a smaller gathering or a meeting with their team (or between both teams), wait for the host to do the honours.

Although Hong Kong Chinese names are usually presented as a surname followed by two linked forenames on their business card, junior members of the team may introduce themselves by more Westernized 'adopted' names such as as 'Kitty' or 'Mandy' or 'Mike'. It is best not to use these names at an early stage in the relationship, unless specifically invited to do so.

Business card etiquette is much the same in Hong Kong as if the rest of Asia. Present the card in both hands with the traditional Chinese translation uppermost and the characters facing your counterpart. When receiving a card, take it formally in two hands and don't slip it into a back pocket. Read it carefully, register the title, and don't write on it. Your business card should also show your job title, thereby allowing your Hong Kong counterparts to understand your place in your company's hierarchy. Be respectful with it.

Saving or losing face

The concept of face is a tricky one but it is essential to try and understand what it entails. Generally speaking, throughout Asia it is a very bad idea to lose your temper or ruffle the surface of business relationships in any way. Collectivism, teamwork, harmony: call it what you will, a Westerner upsetting the apple cart can only expect dire consequences. In Hong Kong, as in other Asian societies, losing face, saving face or (more difficult) *giving* face to another person or company is central to the way business and social relationships work.

But it's not easy to work out when you are doing or not doing it. Recently I was involved in a business tender in Hong Kong that eventually fizzled out because the Hong Kong client did not want to accept my quotation. In Western societies, you would expect to be told this, especially if you were approached first. You could then perhaps negotiate (as I attempted do by e-mail). But by the time an impasse had been reached, after perhaps two weeks, my potential Hong Kong client had clearly decided that to reply in any shape or form was to lose face.

And so by not answering my requests for an update or even for a straightforward refusal, my potential client was (a) saving her company's face (b) saving my face because I had been refused and would therefore lose face (g) giving me face by not telling me the bad news. You see what a minefield face and all its permutations can be?

In the West, we don't care that all that much about our dignity and prestige in negotiations. We just get on with it: yes or no. In Hong Kong, as elsewhere in Asia, you must always remember not to put your counterpart in a face-losing situation. Contradicting someone openly, criticising them in front of someone else, putting them in awkward situations (such as my tender quotation), or patronising them are a sure way to lose business. Always give face through sincere compliments, showing respect or doing something that raises self-esteem.

Dining etiquette

There are thousands of restaurants in Hong Kong, international and Chinese. Dining out is not a very formal experience, although there are certain rules of etiquette—particularly if you are being hosted in a Chinese restaurant.

Generally speaking, it is wise to watch what the others do and do likewise. Don't just sit down but wait to be directed to your seat. Often the foreign guest is placed in a seat of honour next to the host. If it's a Chinese meal, there will be a series of dishes placed on the central revolving dais. Both spoons and chopsticks will be available next to your plate and bowl. Use the chopsticks (if you are able) to pick morsels from the central plateau and place in your bowl. Return the chopsticks to the curved rest every now and then, but don't lay them across your bowl.

The rice comes later, so you are free to use the bowl for eating and to place any bones etc. on your side plate. Only begin eating after the host has begun and if you are offered a morsel by your host or another Hong Kong Chinese, be sure to accept it and eat it with our without rice. However, don't attempt to finish all the dishes on the table or go for a second serving and only use your spoon to scoop up food if and when necessary. Eating everything implies there is not enough food, quite apart from you appearing greedy.

Each course is announced with a toast of *Gan-pai* ('cheers') that is echoed round the table. Raise your glass at the others and join in the toast. Similarly, raise your glass modestly if you are toasted. You may offer a toast yourself if the occasions demands, but only at the end of the meal. As a rule Hong Kong Chinese are not big drinkers with food, preferring to drink tea, so you won't have to be on your guard for excessive tippling as is the case on the Mainland.

If tea is poured into your cup by others, tent your index and second finger on the table top and tap them a couple of times to express thanks. This gesture is widespread in China and even elsewhere, so don't believe the mythical story of its origins in 'kowtowing' to the colonial masters. Finally, don't insist on paying. That would definitely cause the host to lose face!

Building for the long term

One of the major characteristics of Hong Kong is the emphasis placed on family relationships, which is reflected in the number of family-owned companies that have often been founded by entrepreneurs like Li ka-shing fleeing from communist China. It is inevitable that personal relationships played and still play a vital role in these enterprises.

If you want to work together with a Hong Kong businessperson, it is important to aim for a long-term relationship. I have worked with several Hong Kong companies and institutions for a decade or more, and in several cases for much longer than that. These relationships are built not so much on personal rapport, although that might be a contributing factor, but mainly on trust, delivery and respect.

Since Hong Kong people are used to Westerners, they have no problem with directness and long-term relationships are often developed from simple small talk, a fair amount of knowledge of your background, and sometimes on questions that are so personal they almost seem funny. No disrespect is intended, but by asking about family and wife and children in a light-hearted manner, Hong Kong business people are simply trying to discover if they will be comfortable working with you. They will not be comfortable with ironic or sarcastic answers. So avoid these at all costs.

They will also not be comfortable with saying no, which brings us back to the question of face. It's better to say silent, or to allow your partner to be silent, than to fill the 'yes-no' gaps in business conversation. Asians, particularly perhaps those with a Buddhist background, have no problem with the occasional silence.

Gifts and festivals

The Hong Kong calendar is full of festive occasions. Once you are accepted as a long-term business partner, it is inevitable that you will be asked to attend some of these occasions. If you attend, just remember some basic rules and prepare yourself beforehand.

If it's Chinese New Year and you are invited to someone's house on the third or fourth day (two days are for the extended family network), take along some carefully wrapped candies or chocolate or a basket of fruit. Red and gold are auspicious colours for Chinese New Year and other seasons, so choose red or gold wrapping paper. Gifts for other occasions can include alcohol such as plum wine for women and cognac for men, flowers (not white since they suggest mourning), and Asian delicacies such as rice cakes.

At Chinese New Year, give red packets (*lai see*) to employees, service staff at your apartment, juniors and children. Never give clocks or watches, as they are associated with death, or anything that cuts because scissors and knives suggest terminating the relationship. Also avoid anything that comes in fours (the word for four is *say* in Cantonese, meaning death). However, giving eight of something is considered extremely lucky. Gifts are not usually opened when received.

Business meetings and negotiations

Always make an appointment and arrive on time. If you are unavoidably late, telephone the person you are meeting before the meeting is scheduled to start. The most senior person in your team should be introduced first. It may appear that negotiations are slow and detailed but the process is usually highly efficient. It is best not to respond with any sign of impatience or frustration.

Decisions are taken at the very top of the company, possibly not by anyone seated in the room with you. However, this makes for more rapid decisions than in most Asian countries and it results in ready cooperation from all levels of the company below the decision-maker.

One important caveat: the Hong Kong Chinese make decisions largely based on price rather than on the best quality available, so you should always come in with a price that is at the top of the range. It is almost certain that they will not accept that price. A surprising number of business decisions are made on a meeting-halfway basis, which leaves everyone happy and more importantly, face is saved all round.

Taiwan

The business culture of Taiwan is not very different from that of Hong Kong. However, there are some important variants.

Largely based on the Kuomintang supporters that escaped the communists in Mainland China before 1949, Taiwan's population of some 24 million is mostly Han Chinese who were born on the Mainland or have ancestors from there. They are divided into three groups based on the Chinese dialect they speak: Taiwanese, Hakka, and Mandarin. Taiwan also has a small population of aborigines that comprise about two per cent of the total population. English is the most popular foreign language in Taiwan and is part of the regular school curriculum. The form of government is multi-party democracy.

Confucianism and the family

As in Hong Kong, many people in Taiwan base their values on Confucian ethics, although these are tempered by close ties with America and by rapid modernization. Traditional values include respect for parents, ancestor worship, a strong emphasis on work and education, a sense of belonging to a wider community, and an aversion to losing 'face'.

Taiwan is also a democratic and modern society in which women enjoy greater freedom and a higher social status than in many Asian countries. Innovation and individuality are regarded as just as valuable as social conformity (an unusual trait in Asian countries) while the status that comes from acquiring material goods has become a significant driver of social mobility.

Building for the long term

Mutual trust and reputation are key to building long-term relationships in Taiwan. Connections (*guanxi*) are extremely important. In Europe and US, when people do business they begin to socialize with each other over time. However, in Taiwan people who know each other socially or through the family often do business together. This means that trust of outsiders has to be very carefully built.

In negotiations, people that share a common background are a much stronger determinant of the outcome than questions of price. Many negotiations in Taiwan are carried out in social clubs for Chinese, Japanese and Taiwanese. Even in high-tech businesses, partnerships are largely formed between classmates or army pals or family relations.

Indeed, the Taiwanese only really trust themselves or their immediate family. The owner of the business (rather than the CEO) does everything through social and familial contacts. Opportunities for outsiders are therefore limited, especially if they are not a company owner themselves.

Saving or losing face

Taiwanese have high expectations of how they will be treated, especially in relation to 'face'. Face issues influence how the Taiwanese negotiate. They don't believe in win-win results of negotiations; they must feel that they have won even if the outcome is not necessarily the best deal for them. On the other hand, within the charmed circle of trust, even verbal agreements can last for years between both individuals and companies.

The focus on 'face' also means that the Taiwanese are highly competitive, beginning at school. Big businesses are riddled with competition between small groups, but this ruthless competitiveness is focused largely on other Taiwanese. What may seem to be an old-fashioned prejudice towards 'foreign devils' (the Cantonese expression for foreigners) often turns out to be a preference for foreign partners rather than for Taiwanese competitors. So despite all the odds, there are opportunities for Westerners in the Taiwan market.

It is easy for a Westerner to tap into this by praising almost any aspect of a company or group or the country as a whole. You can give yourself additional face by presenting letters of introduction from well-known business leaders, overseas Taiwanese or former government officials who have dealt with Taiwan. Above all, make sure you or your representative remain the face of your company over a considerable period so that your Taiwanese partners can learn to trust you. Do not chop and change personnel.

Gifts and festivals

Like Hong Kong, the Taiwanese calendar is full of festive occasions. Once you are accepted as being a long-term business partner, it is inevitable that you will be asked to attend some of these occasions. If you attend, just remember some basic rules and prepare yourself beforehand.

If it's Chinese New Year and you are invited to someone's house on the third or fourth day (two days are for the extended family network), take along some carefully wrapped candies or chocolate or a basket of fruit. Red and gold are auspicious colours for Chinese New Year and other seasons, so choose red or gold wrapping paper. Gifts for other occasions can include alcohol such as plum wine for women and cognac for men, flowers (not white since they imply death), and Asian delicacies such as Japanese rice cakes.

At Chinese New Year, give red packets (*lai see*) to employees, service staff at your apartment, juniors and children. Never give clocks or watches, as they are associated with death, or anything that cuts because scissors and knives suggest terminating the relationship. Also avoid anything that comes in fours (the word for four is *say* in Cantonese, meaning death). However, giving eight of something is considered extremely lucky. Gifts are not usually opened when received.

Meeting and greeting

The Taiwanese shake hands with a nod of the head. They don't tend to stare you straight in the eye and they won't expect you to obviously analyse or eyeball them during the meeting. If it's a large reception you may have to introduce yourself to the other guests but at a smaller gathering or a meeting with their team (or between both teams), wait for the host to do the honours.

Taiwanese names are usually presented as a surname followed by two linked forenames on their business card, junior members of the team may introduce themselves by more Westernized 'adopted' names'. It is best not to use these names at an early stage in the relationship, unless specifically invited to do so. Let your card do the talking.

Business card etiquette is much the same in Taiwan as in the rest of Asia. Present the card in both hands with the traditional Chinese translation uppermost and the characters facing your counterpart. Seek advice from a local person about Chinese characters with the most favourable connotations (Western names can be translated in different ways).

When receiving a card, take it formally in two hands and don't slip it into a back pocket. Read it carefully, register the title, and don't write on it. Your business card should also show your job title, thereby allowing your Taiwanese counterparts to understand your place in your company's hierarchy. Be respectful with it.

Dining etiquette

The Taiwanese prefer to eat out in restaurants rather than entertain at home. Dining out is not a very formal experience, although there are certain rules of etiquette—particularly if you are being hosted in a Chinese restaurant.

Generally speaking, it is wise to watch what the others do and do likewise. Don't just sit down but wait to be directed to your seat. Often the foreign guest is placed in a seat of honour next to the host. If it's a Chinese meal, there will be a series of dishes placed on the central revolving dais. Both spoons and chopsticks will be available next to your plate and bowl. Use the chopsticks (if you are able) to pick morsels from the central plateau and place in your bowl. Return the chopsticks to the curved rest every now and then, but don't lay them across your bowl.

The rice comes later, so you are free to use the bowl for eating and to place any bones etc. on your side plate. Only begin eating after the host has begun and if you are offered a morsel by your host or another Taiwanese at the table, be sure to accept it and eat it with our without rice. However, don't attempt to finish all the dishes on the table or go for a second serving and only use your spoon to scoop up food if and when necessary. Eating everything implies there is not enough food, quite apart from you appearing greedy.

If a course is announced with a toast, raise your glass with the others and join in. Similarly, raise your glass modestly if you are toasted. You may offer a toast yourself if the occasion demands, but only at the end of the meal. As a rule the Taiwanese are not big drinkers with food, preferring to drink tea, so you won't have to be on your guard for excessive tippling as is sometimes the case on the Mainland.

Business meetings and negotiations

Taiwanese business meetings are not particularly formal, nor time-conscious. However, the Taiwanese do appreciate in-depth information. They also appreciate it if you send along your most senior person to represent the company. The Chinese admire age and status.

It is best to provide a well-crafted and fairly lengthy opening statement for business meetings in Taiwan, preferably translated into Chinese. This can provide an agenda, or more likely the outline for an agenda that can take off in various directions, including some non-business conversation. The Taiwanese approach is first to obtain an overall view of the proposal, then to focus on concrete issues. Once the overseas team has laid out its position, the Taiwanese leader will respond in a dialogue that becomes less open-ended and more focused.

Directness and clarity are appreciated in the statement, but from then onwards it is important to avoid placing any Taiwanese member of the team in a face-losing position. Proposals are made obliquely and carefully, and silence is preferred to any open disagreement. Avoid exerting pressure or saying no directly. Learn to use subtle expressions such as 'maybe' or a nod of the head, both of which probably mean no. Emphasize the compatibility of your two companies, your desire to work with your counterpart, and your sincerity.

Singapore

Singapore has made great strides since independence from Britain in 1965, both as an economy and as a nation. In terms of purchasing power parity, Singapore has the third highest per capita income in the world. There are slightly over 5 million people in Singapore, of which almost 3 million were born locally. The population is highly diverse; the majority is Chinese, and Malays and Indians form significant minorities. Reflecting this diversity, the country has four official languages: English, Mandarin, Malay, and Tamil. For business and politics, English is the language of choice.

The family

The family is the focus of most social life and behaviour in every ethnic group. This includes members of the nuclear or extended family, which often live apart due to the restricted space on such a small island. Elderly family members are highly respected, many businesses flourish on patriarchies, and there is a strong culture of collectivism. Clearly, due to the variety of ethnic groups, there are gradations in beliefs and behaviour between families of different ethnic backgrounds.

Muslim and Indian women, for example, are not as involved in business and public life as Chinese women (fuller comparisons can be made by referring to the sections on China and Malaysia). In general, Singaporean society is polite, conservative and reserved, whatever the eccentricities of the younger generation (which still tends to defer to family and authority).

Saving or losing face

Face is what makes Singaporeans strive for harmonious relationships. Face can extend to family, ethnic background, school, company, and the nation itself. Although there is tolerance and encouragement of ethnic and religious activities, any hint of ethnic divisions is feared and avoided. The emphasis on the common language of English, and the education system combine to make Singaporeans think of themselves as Singaporean first and of their ethnic background second.

Face also extends beyond personal behaviour to inappropriate comments such as jokes with a sexual or political meaning. Comments on national politics or religious issues are particularly to be avoided, as is any complaint about the laws. Some of these are quite surprising for Westerners, such as those against chewing gum, littering, spitting or jaywalking. But Singaporeans believe they are responsible for the high standards of order and cleanliness in this island nation. Don't criticize.

Meeting and greeting

The three main ethnic groups are religiously and culturally diverse. This extends to meeting and greeting. Younger people or those who work in Western companies usually adopt the Western practice of shaking hands with everyone, but this is not the case with older or more reserved Singaporeans. Ethnic Chinese shake hands lightly as in Hong Kong and Taiwan, although the woman must extend her hand first.

Between men, ethnic Malays shake hands but men and women traditionally do not since Muslim men do not touch women in public. These days younger Malays shake hands with both Western men and women, even if it is more traditional to use a 'salaam' (bowing of the head) to women.

Muslims, especially Malays, touch their chests after shaking hands to symbolize that the greeting comes from the heart. They are pleased when the foreigner returns the gesture. Ethnic Indians shake hands with members of the same sex. Nodding of the head and smiling is more usual when being introduced to someone of the opposite sex.

Names and titles

Chinese

Chinese names in Singapore are the same as in the rest of the Chinese world. The surname or family name comes first, followed by two personal names. A Westerner should address a Chinese by their honorific title and their surname. If the Chinese person wants to move to a first name basis in business, they will advise you. Don't take it for granted.

Malay

Many Malays do not have surnames. Instead, men add the father's name to their own name with the connector 'bin' (son of). Sufyan Adli becomes Sufyan Adli bin Supiani. Women use the connector 'binti' (daughter of). The title Haji (male) or Hajjah (female) before the name indicates the person has made a pilgrimage to Mecca. The name Sayyed (male) or Sharifah (female) indicates that the person is considered to be a descendant of the prophet Mohammed.

Indian

Many Indians in Singapore do not use surnames. Instead, they place the initial of their father's name in front of their own name. Since many Indian names are extremely long, they commonly use a shortened version of their name as a sort of nickname. Sikh Indians all use the name Singh to denote themselves as Sikhs.

Business cards

Business card etiquette is much the same in Singapore as if the rest of Asia. Present the card in both hands with the English or Chinese translation uppermost and the characters facing your counterpart (depending on the ethnic background of the recipient). When receiving a card, take it formally in two hands and don't slip it into a back pocket. Read it carefully, register the title, and don't write on it. Your business card should also show your job title, thereby allowing your Singaporean counterparts to understand your place in your company's hierarchy. Be respectful with it.

Gifts and festivals

The three main ethnic groups treat gift-giving in a different manner. If you are invited to an ethnic Chinese home for dinner, take along some carefully wrapped candies or chocolate or a basket of fruit. Red and gold are auspicious colours for wrapping. Gifts can include alcohol such as plum wine for women and cognac for men, cakes and delicacies not usually found in Singapore. At Chinese New Year, give red packets (*lai see*) to employees, service staff at your apartment, juniors and children.

Never give clocks or watches, as they are associated with death, or anything that cuts because scissors and knives suggest terminating the relationship. However, giving eight of something is considered extremely lucky. Gifts are not usually opened when received.

Ethnic Malays prefer gifts on parting rather than on arrival. Do not try to give alcohol, anything associated with pigs or pork or anything wrapped in white (the colour of death). Gifts of food should be halal. Offer gifts with the right hand or both hands. Gifts are not opened when received.

Flowers are appreciated as gifts by ethnic Indians, but avoid frangipani since it is used in funeral wreaths. Unlike for the Chinese, money should be given in odd numbers. Wrap gifts in bright colours, not in white or black. Do not give alcohol unless the recipient is known to like it. Gifts are not opened when received.

Business meetings and negotiations

Always make an appointment and arrive on time. If you are unavoidably late, telephone the person you are meeting before the meeting is scheduled to start. The most senior person in your team should be introduced first to his or her counterpart in the Singaporean group, since rank and age are observed in a strict chain of command. The group (company or department) is viewed as more important than the individual.

Long-standing personal relationships or the proper introductions will eventually assure you are tied into the network, which is often based on educational or ethnic links or simply working for the same company. These relationships take time to develop; don't be impatient or show frustration. Once you are recognized as part of the group, you will be accepted and expected to obey the unwritten rules of the group. Decisions are taken at the very top of the company based on consensus, possibly not by anyone seated in the room with you.

They will be based on rationality and the amount of information your Singaporean counterparts have been given. However, since a straightforward 'no' will be avoided to save face, it will not be immediately apparent what those decisions may be. Much communication is non-verbal. You will have to closely watch the facial expressions and body language of people you work with for any indications.

Remember that Singaporeans are tough negotiators on price and deadlines. Only through patience and asking indirect questions (perhaps over a period of time) can progress be monitored and possible agreement ratified. Don't try to fill the silence after a question or an awkward pause after a presentation. Such pauses may indicate careful thought! Singaporeans believe that Westerners' haste to answer questions shows thoughtlessness or even rudeness.

Japan

Almost the entire 128 million population of Japan is ethnic Japanese, the remaining being mainly Ainu and Koreans. There is a strong division of attitude towards things (and people) of Japanese origin and those of foreign origin. The Japanese word for a foreigner is *gaijin*, meaning 'outsider'. Since Japanese is the only language spoken, with some local variants, and English is only attempted by those ready to make mistakes in public and by some of the more internet-savvy of the younger generation, the division between Japanese and foreigner sometimes seems like a chasm.

However, many business people are now more cosmopolitan and used to foreign travel or running Japanese companies abroad, so the cultural gap is not quite so yawning as it once was.

Japanese beliefs and the family

Buddhism and Shintoism are the main Japanese religions, teaching harmony within society and respect for nature. Confucianism and ancestor worship have also influenced Japanese society, emphasizing strong family obligations and loyalty, social hierarchy (the Japanese are extremely conscious of age and status), ritualistic behavior and politeness.

In Japan 'we' comes before 'I' and there is little reward for individuality. The Japanese educational system emphasizes the interdependence of all people, and Japanese children are not raised to be independent but rather to work together. This is reflected in the consensus building and fixed hierarchical relationships that are among the most important traits of Japanese culture and business culture. Although younger professionals exposed to Western values are trying to demonstrate more individuality and independence within both business and social life, these changes do not yet extend in a significant way to the family.

Meeting and greeting

Japan is a very deferential and polite society, which means that greetings are also both formal and ritualized. Everyone knows the image of the Japanese bowing to each other in the street or in a shop, even in a foreign country. This bowing comes from a strong sense of respect and an adherence to an 'image' or 'symbol' of politeness that can mask many nuances of meaning beneath the surface.

Westerners are not expected to bow except perhaps with a slight forward tilt of the head, but only to shake hands (lightly). Similarly, it is not expected that foreigners introduce themselves at business receptions but rather that they should wait to be introduced, preferably by presenting their business card.

The emphasis on the group and not on the individual inclines the Japanese towards dependence on facial expression, tone of voice and posture to convey the responses they feel. The context or the situation is as important as the words expressed, which is why the Japanese are considered to be 'impassive' while speaking and why they often maintain their privacy in public by avoiding eye contact. This non-verbal communication is so deep-rooted that it has spawned a cottage industry of books for Westerners to get to know the important signs!

Business cards

The Japanese are high-frequency exchangers of business cards, which they do with much formality. As in China, Hong Kong and Taiwan, make sure your business cards are high quality, in perfect condition and translated into the local language, in this case Japanese.

Present the business card with two hands, a slight incline of the head and with the Japanese characters facing the recipient. You should include your title on the card, since the Japanese recipient will want to know your status and position in your company's hierarchy. When receiving a card, take it formally in two hands and don't slip it into a back pocket. Read it carefully, register the title, and don't write on it. During a meeting, place the business cards on the table in front of you and refer to them when your Japanese counterparts are speaking.

Saving or losing face

Saving face and maintaining dignity are crucial in Japanese society. Japanese will avoid at all costs drawing attention to anything that might cause embarrassment to themselves or others. Their style of communication relies heavily on non-verbal, intuitive clues, or what they call *haragei* (literally, 'art of the stomach'). As a result they are not likely to act spontaneously or to openly refuse a request.

Tactics used to avoid confrontation include a prolonged silence in business meetings, which can be both positive or negative; a hissing sound made by drawing in air through the teeth ('this is going to be difficult for me'); and avoidance of questions, which allows Japanese to 'read between the lines' rather than rely on Q&As and clear statements like Westerners.

In general, Japanese will find a way to avoid saying 'no' or to openly criticize or praise any individual if it means they are singled out from the group. In a culture that stresses interdependence and collectivism independent thinkers are not encouraged. The result is that the Japanese tend to be rather rule bound, highly methodical and fastidious in their daily activities. Bending rules is tantamount to losing face, which is the overriding social factor.

Dining etiquette

Business lunches and dinners are common and are good times to get to know your Japanese counterparts. The Japanese trust those with whom they socialize so never turn down an after-hours invitation. But be careful not to disclose too much or become over-personal (despite the beer and saké flowing!).

Evening dining and drinking are considered to be part of the workday for male professionals, but strictly without the wife. However, more and more women professionals now take part in the drinking before the meal, the meal itself, and the often inevitable karaoke afterwards. The key to all three events is participation. You don't have to be champion drinker, or a lover of sushi and sashimi, or an Elton John or Liza Minelli. You just have to take part.

Generally speaking, in the restaurant it is wise to watch what the others do and do likewise. Don't just sit down but wait to be directed to your seat. Often the foreign guest is placed in a seat of honour next to or opposite the host. Only begin eating after the host has begun. Both spoons and chopsticks will be available next to your plate and bowl. Use the chopsticks (if you are able) to pick morsels from the dish placed in front of you. Don't mix the delicacies in the rice as is the practice in Chinese countries, unless the dish is already a mixture such as broiled eel and rice. Return the chopsticks to the curved rest every now and then, but don't lay them across your bowl.

Don't pierce the food with the chopsticks. They are thinner and more delicate than the Chinese variety, which is appropriate for the 'painterly' and aesthetic nature of Japanese cuisine. Even if you hate raw fish try just a little and go for the rice and warmer dishes instead. If you finish your rice, your bowl will probably be refilled. The same goes for your glass, so leave something in it if you want to stay sober. However, don't attempt to finish all the dishes on the table or go for a second serving. Eating everything implies there is not enough food, quite apart from you appearing greedy. Don't be surprised if your Japanese colleagues slurp their noodles and soup; this implies pleasure and is taken as a compliment.

The Japanese will rarely invite you home, since Japanese homes are small and crowded. If you do go, remember to remove your shoes before entering and leave them at the doorway facing the exit. You will usually be provided with slippers, and there will be another pair of rubber slippers in the bathroom if you use the toilet (remember to leave them there!).

A gift should be taken, but not flowers. Department stores in Japan are full of delicate gifts in attractive packaging for just such occasions. If your host has a tatami (straw mat) floor, the men will sit cross-legged at the low table on the tatami while the women kneel.

Offer your glass for refilling by holding it at the stem. You may also politely refill your hosts' glasses by holding the bottle in two hands and delicately pouring. If you are not a close friend, dress as conservatively as you would for any business meeting. Jackets can be discarded when the meal is in full flow.

Building for the long term

The Japanese prefer to do business on the basis of personal relationships. An experienced Western executive will find out who the key decision-makers are for a particular project after liaising with outside intermediaries that have a good relationship with people within the company itself.

This does not mean that the deal will be done. It is essential to connect with other people in planning, manufacturing, marketing and so on in order to build consensus. This means that a lot of patience is required; local knowledge and well respected local contacts must be nurtured over a long period.

Good written communication is essential, which means that you must use writers that have knowledge of Japan's strict cultural protocols. The Westerner is allowed to make mistakes because he or she is not conversant with Japanese. This is tolerated as long as genuine respect is shown.

Gifts and festivals

Vast amounts of money are spent in Japan each year on gifts. Some of these gifts are tantamount to bribes but others are given because of obligation or duty, or as thank you's or condolences, or simply to mark a festival or seasonal events such as midsummer or New Year's Day.

The Japanese place great emphasis on the way a gift is wrapped or presented, often more than on the gift itself. It is best to ask someone knowledgeable about these customs to help you decide what gift to give and how it should be presented. High quality chocolates or 'foreign' delicacies are welcome. Avoid anything associated with funerals such as white lilies, camellias or lotus blossoms.

Business meetings and negotiations

Few Japanese understand English well, so it is important to provide written information in both English and Japanese on your company, your proposal and what your clients have said about you both for use at the meeting and prior to it. The quality of your presentation and material will reveal to the Japanese the standards of your company, its reliability and products. Since this is a group society, at your first meeting your Japanese counterpart will probably be accompanied by several associates.

The place of honour is usually the furthest from the door. Make a good show of refusing this honour if you are offered such a place. In order to develop the relationship, the Japanese may go through a series of 'getting to know you' questions before shifting the conversation towards business. This initial social interaction is part of the long-term process of building a successful relationship, allowing your Japanese counterparts to eventually become comfortable enough to do business with you.

Do not refuse any requests for a small amount of business to begin with; it will be a trial of your ability and trustworthiness. At the end of the meeting, always offer a small gift as a token of esteem to the most senior person. Don't be put off if your Japanese counterparts remain silent for long periods of time, or by their closing their eyes when they are listening intently. They are not going to sleep! They are concentrating.

Always remain polite and soft-spoken and expect only incremental progress. As a general rule, the Japanese do not see contracts as final and they will prefer a broad mutual understanding so that the essential element of flexibility can be maintained.

South Korea

South Korea, the Republic of Korea (ROK), occupies the southern half of the Korean Peninsula while communist North Korea, which is perennially on the edge of economic collapse, forms the larger northern half. Following the Korean War in 1953, a buffer zone called the Demilitarized Zone (DMZ) was set up as a boundary between North and South Korea. Seoul, the capital of South Korea, is just 35 miles south of the DMZ. With its population of almost 50 million people, South Korea is one of the most densely populated nations in the world.

After the Korean War, South Koreans steadily rebuilt their country into 'The Miracle of the Han River'. World-class steel, automotive, marine transport, semiconductors and telecommunications industries have flourished in recent decades alongside the transition from a military government to an open and democratic political system, and from dependence on manufacturing exports to high value-added, well-designed and capital-intensive products.

The years of Japanese colonial rule from 1910 to 1945 and the constant threats from North Korea have forged a national identity and work ethic that combine well with Korea's ancient Confucian roots to create a unique world view and robust business culture.

Confucianism and the family

Koreans are an emotional and spiritual people. A quarter of the population is practising Buddhist (many more are non-practising Buddhist), a quarter is Christian, and at least as many believe in the shamanist principle that the world is inhabited by spirits that live in nature and that can be summoned or placated through rituals involving incantation, music and dance.

Woven into all these beliefs is a powerful strand of Confucianism, which emphasizes the importance of family, the authority of elders and of ancestor worship. As in many Asian societies, eldest sons are expected to financially support the family and to carry on the family name by marrying and having sons of their own.

Children are raised to believe they can never repay their debt to their parents, hence the popularity of ancestor worship. Ancestral ceremonies for the previous three generations (parents, grandparents, and great grandparents) are held several times a year. The many burial mounds that dot the countryside testify to the long lineage of Korean families, some of which can trace their family's history back to male ancestors some 500 years ago.

Meeting and greeting

There are rules of protocol when greeting a Korean but they are not quite so set in stone as those in Japan. The Koreans are generally more relaxed about such procedures. A person of lower status bows to a person of higher status but the most senior person will offer the handshake that follows after the bow (a good example of the Korean taste for mix-and-match). They will say 'pleased to meet you' in Korean but unless you are fluent in their language, don't try to reply. A smile and a handshake usually do the trick, plus a business card.

However, make sure that you wait to be introduced at a social gathering and when you leave, say good-bye and try to give a short bow (not a Mr. Bean parody) to everyone present. Remember that women also require a handshake and bow, although the Confucian ethic still relegates women to a lower position in Korean society than men. Women usually appear quiet and submissive in public. In reality, women wield considerable power behind the scenes, often managing the family finances and wellbeing and they are increasingly visible at management level. Don't be fooled by the Korean male walking through the door ahead of his wife and her helping him into his coat!

An interesting difference to other Asian countries is that Koreans may very well look you straight in the eye when presenting themselves. There's a surprising directness in the Korean approach to outsiders. This is possibly explained by the extreme emphasis Koreans place on the importance of the visual. As outlined in Step Two, Koreans will draw initial conclusions about you based also entirely on what you look like. Remember to keep up your standards of personal branding so that your project the kind of stylishness, confidence and culture that is so much part of modern Korean life.

Business card etiquette in Korea is much the same as in the rest of Asia. Present the card in both hands with the Korean translation uppermost and the characters facing your counterpart. When receiving a card, take it formally in two hands and don't slip it into a back pocket. Read it carefully, register the title, and don't write on it. Your business card should also show your job title, thereby allowing your Korean counterparts to understand your place in your company's hierarchy. Be respectful with it.

Saving or losing face

In South Korea, as in other Asian societies, face is central to the way business and social relationships work. Through their social etiquette and behaviour, Koreans aim to preserve a harmonious environment in which a person's *kibun* can remain balanced. *Kibun* literally means mood or inner feelings.

Any damage to *kibun* damages the business relationship. This means that Koreans often appear helpful, polite and friendly on a personal level but they will aim to do nothing that upsets *kibun*, such as middle management always saying 'yes' when they mean 'no', never giving a straight answer, never assuming personal responsibility for anything. The best way to handle *kibun* is not to demand yes or no answers, as in Japan, and to accept the need for slow consensual decision-making.

Given Korea's history of subjugation, it is vital to treat South Koreans with proper respect and to avoid any situation in which they or their country might appear to lose face. Contradicting people openly, criticising them in front of someone else or patronising them are a sure way to lose business. Always give face through sincere compliments, showing respect or doing something that raises self-esteem.

Dining etiquette

There are certain rules of etiquette if you are invited to dine in a Korean restaurant. Generally speaking, it is wise to watch what the others do and do likewise. Don't just sit down but wait to be directed to your seat. Often the foreign guest is placed in a seat of honour next to the host. If it's a Korean meal, there will usually be a series of largely vegetarian dishes (*namul*) and spicy pickled cabbage (*kimchi*) placed centrally on the table as an accompaniment to barbecued meat or fish or chicken.

Both soup spoons and metal chopsticks will be available next to your plate and rice bowl. Use the chopsticks (if you are able) to pick morsels from the central dishes and place in your bowl. Return the chopsticks to the curved rest every now and then, but don't lay them across your bowl.

Only begin eating after the host has begun. At the end of the meal you will be served fruit, which should be eaten with the toothpick provided. South Koreans are lively hosts and like their beer and *soju* (high-proof potato wine), so be warned. When I worked as a columnist for a national Korean magazine, I lost count of the number of times I was *soju-ed* by the end of the evening.

If you are invited to a South Korean's house, it is usual for guests to meet at a common spot and travel together because of the distances involved in big cities and the difficulty of finding private houses. Try to be reasonably on time and remove your shoes in the hallway before entering the house. You will probably by offered the same *namul* vegetarian dishes (Buddhist in origin) that you receive in a restaurant, so pick your favourites and go easy with anything you don't really like.

The host will pour you a drink from a bottle with the left hand supporting the right forearm and gently inclining the bottle towards your glass, which you should raise from the table. Be sure to reciprocate the gesture in the same elegant way; it is Confucian good manners. The hosts usually accompany guests to the gate or to their car because they believe that it is impolite to bid guests farewell indoors. Be sure to send a thank you note the following day.

Building for the long term

One of the major characteristics of South Korea is the emphasis placed on family relationships, which is reflected in the number of family-owned companies that have often been founded by entrepreneurs and that have remained essentially patriarchal in nature. It is inevitable that personal relationships played and still play a vital role in these enterprises.

If you want to work together with a South Korean businessperson, it is important to aim for a long-term relationship. Profit will often not be the only motivator for a Korean business partner. Like the Japanese, the Korean is concerned with market share and growth. This means that making a quick buck before exiting is not a good negotiating approach.

Family-owned Korean businesses can take the long-term view, unlike a Western company with shareholders demanding their profits in the short term. It is best to begin on the periphery of the business relationship and gradually focus in on the main business in decreasing circles. Koreans view impatience as a major fault, so be sure not to go immediately to the core of the project.

Gifts and festivals

The South Korean calendar is full of festive occasions. Once you are accepted as being a long-term business partner, it is inevitable that you will be asked to attend some of these occasions. If you attend, just remember some basic rules and prepare yourself beforehand.

If you are invited to someone's house, for example for Buddha's Birthday or *Chusok* (Korean Thanksgiving Day), take along some carefully wrapped candies or chocolate or a basket of fruit. Red and gold are royal colours while yellow or pink denote happiness, so choose your wrapping paper accordingly. Gifts can include alcohol such as plum wine for women and cognac for men, flowers (not white since they suggest mourning), and Asian delicacies. Avoid anything that comes in fours. However, the number seven is considered extremely lucky. Gifts are not usually opened when received.

Business meetings and negotiations

Always make an appointment and arrive on time. If you are unavoidably late, telephone the person you are meeting before the meeting is scheduled to start. The most senior person in your team should be introduced first. It may appear that negotiations are proceeding very slowly but the main purpose of the first meeting is to get to know each other as he foundation for building a further relationship. It is best not to respond with any sign of impatience or frustration.

Make sure that all your materials, client testimonials and company information are in both English and Korean (more Koreans in the big cities and in business now speak English, but fluency cannot be taken for granted) and that they are sent to the South Korean side beforehand along with an agenda.

As mentioned above, South Koreans like direct communication. They will ask precise questions if they do not understand what has been said or need additional clarification. They should be answered in a similar, straightforward manner. Avoid 'yes-no' questions and aim to develop the relationship for the long term. Mutual trust and understanding will come about through a series of social gatherings that involve a good deal of eating, drinking and possibly karaoke. Like the Japanese, South Koreans view the contracts that rise from such relationships as loosely structured consensus statements that broadly define agreement and leave room for flexibility and adjustment as needed.

The developing economies – China, Philippines, Malaysia, Indonesia, Thailand, Vietnam

China

China is the most populous country in the world with approximately 1.3 billion people. Han Chinese constitute around 92 per cent of the population with the rest being made up of more than 55 minority groups. It is important to remember that even within the Han Chinese there are significant differences in language and dialects, social customs, physical features and attitudes.

There are four main religions and beliefs that dominate Chinese life and values: Confucianism, Buddhism, Taoism and ancestor worship (some would say communism and materialism too, or at least the contemporary fusion of the two). Of these it is Confucianism that has exercised the greatest influence on the way Chinese behave, especially in regard to the family, respect for elders, deference to authority and consciousness of rank.

Confucianism and the family

Confucianism is a system of ethics that stress the obligations of people towards one another based upon their relationship. Most of these relationships are familial but not all; the respect of subject for ruler is also based on obligation and duty. In China, maintaining harmonious relations and stability depends on respect for power and authority. The most distinctive feature of Chinese business is hierarchy, particularly in state-owned enterprises (SOEs), with the Chairman as the all-powerful figure rather like the head of the family.

As a collective society with a need for group affiliation, whether to their family, school, work group, or country, Chinese will strive to act with decorum at all times and will not do anything to cause someone else public embarrassment.

Saving or losing face

In such a collectivist and hierarchical society, it is essential that outsiders avoid causing a Chinese to lose face at any time. The Chinese largely rely on facial expression, tone of voice and posture to tell them what someone feels. If someone disagrees with what another person in a meeting, that person will remain quiet. This gives respect to the other person, whereas speaking out would make both parties lose face.

The direct eye contact used by a Westerner to show interest may be taken as an aggressive tactic by the Chinese who will not look you in the eye when you are talking to them since it is considered rude. Frowning while someone is speaking is also interpreted as a sign of disagreement. Therefore, most Chinese maintain an impassive expression when speaking. However, the Chinese do love to applaud (in the communist style), so don't be surprised if you are greeted at meetings by a round of applause. It is a measure of respect and solidarity and giving face. If it happens, be respectful and applaud back.

Meeting and greeting

Greetings are formal and the oldest person is always greeted first. The Chinese shake hands delicately rather than bowing. They avoid staring you straight in the eye and they will expect you to do the same during the meeting. If it's a large reception you may have to introduce yourself to the other guests but at a smaller gathering or a meeting with their team (or between both teams), wait for the host to do the honours.

Chinese names are usually presented as a surname followed by two linked forenames on their business card. Use the surname with an honorific on first meeting. If your Chinese counterparts want to move to a first-name basis, they will advise you which name to use. Like the Overseas Chinese, Mainland Chinese have a strong sense of humour when they feel comfortable in a relationship. Be prepared to laugh at yourself.

Business card etiquette is much the same as in Hong Kong and Taiwan. Present the card in both hands with the simplified Chinese translation uppermost and the characters facing your counterpart. Take advice on the Chinese characters for your name and title with the most auspicious connotations. When receiving a card, take it formally in two hands and don't slip it into a back pocket. Read it carefully, register the title, and don't write on it. Your business card should also show your job title, thereby allowing your Chinese counterparts to understand your place in your company's hierarchy. Be respectful with it.

Gifts and festivals

The Chinese calendar is full of festive occasions. Once you are accepted as being a long-term business partner, it is inevitable that you will be asked to attend some of these occasions. If you attend, just remember some basic rules and prepare yourself beforehand.

If it's Chinese New Year and you are invited to someone's house on the third or fourth day (two days are for the extended family network), take along some carefully wrapped candies or chocolate or a basket of fruit. Red and gold are auspicious colours for Chinese New Year and other seasons, so choose red or gold wrapping paper. Gifts for other occasions can include alcohol such as plum wine for women and cognac for men, flowers (not white since they suggest mourning), and Asian delicacies.

At Chinese New Year, give red packets (*lai see*) to employees, service staff at your apartment, juniors and children. Never give clocks or watches, as they are associated with death, or anything that cuts because scissors and knives suggest terminating the relationship. Also avoid anything that comes in fours (the word for four is *say* in Cantonese, meaning death). However, giving eight of something is considered extremely lucky.

Gifts are not usually opened when received and they may be refused up to three times before being accepted.

Dining etiquette

The Chinese prefer to entertain in public places rather than in their homes, especially when entertaining foreigners. If you are being hosted in a Chinese restaurant, it is wise to watch what the others do and do likewise. Don't just sit down but wait to be directed to your seat. Often the foreign guest is placed in a seat of honour next to the host.

If it's a Chinese meal, there will be a series of dishes placed on the central revolving dais. Both spoons and chopsticks will be available next to your plate and bowl. Use the chopsticks (if you are able) to pick morsels from the central plateau and place in your bowl. Return the chopsticks to the curved rest every now and then, but don't lay them across your bowl. The rice comes later, so you are free to use the bowl for eating and to place any bones etc. on your side plate. Only begin eating after the host has begun and if you are offered a morsel by your host or another Chinese, be sure to accept it and eat it with our without rice.

However, don't attempt to finish all the dishes on the table or go for a second serving and only use your spoon to scoop up food if and when necessary. Eating everything implies there is not enough food, quite apart from you appearing greedy. Each course may be announced with a toast of *Kam-pei* ('cheers') that is echoed round the table. Raise your glass at the others and join in the toast. Similarly, raise your glass modestly if you are toasted. You may offer a toast yourself if the occasions demands, but only at the end of the meal.

Mainland Chinese can be big drinkers at banquets, so be on your guard for excessive tippling. If tea is poured into your cup by others, tent your index and second finger on the table top and tap them a couple of times to express thanks. Finally, don't insist on paying. That would definitely cause the host to lose face!

If you are invited to a private house, consider it a great honour and be sure to arrive on time. Remove your shoes before entering the house and present a small gift to the hostess. Eat well to demonstrate that you are enjoying the food, but again you don't have to finish everything on the table. Over-abundance shows the status of the host.

Building for the long term

The main business-related cross-cultural difference between the West and the Chinese is the significance of the long-term business relationship. What the Chinese call *guanxi* (relationship) is at the heart of Chinese business deals. When Chinese business people meet for the first time, they begin to immediately build *guanxi*. They will probably spend many hours drinking tea or dining and discussing what seems 'non-business' to Westerners. Chinese use this process to assess people they might like to work with. This often makes results driven Westerners very impatient.

However, having a good network of connections (*guanxi*) in China is the most important element of business success. Every Chinese cultivates his or her own network of personal relationships in business, by which is meant networks with obligations. For Westerners too, *guanxi* relationships and networking often serve to smooth out operations. It is therefore essential to work initially through an intermediary that can make a formal introduction and vouch for the reliability of your company. Team members must be recruited that understand how the *guanxi* system works.

Business relationships are built formally after the Chinese begin to know you through your intermediaries and associates, the materials that describe your company, and face-to-face meetings. Every step along the way is slow, burdened with bureaucracy, and requires extreme patience. But the rewards of persistence can often be highly worthwhile. At no stage in the process should it be forgotten that the correct approach is official and formal. Social events are not the places for business discussion, and the two should not be confused.

Meetings and negotiations

It is important to pave the way for the first negotiation or presentation; to see your Chinese counterparts without a fixed agenda. This can take several months. Older Chinese can attend whole meetings without a substantive issue being discussed. Trust has to develop before bargaining begins. When negotiations finally occur, the Chinese do not necessarily pursue a win-win line, but rather one of 'fair play' for those that have dealings with them.

They are particularly attracted to value-enhancing investors, such as those with expertise in accounting, marketing and technical systems and know-how. Ultimately, they tend to look for *good long-term relationships*. Once you reach the negotiating or presentation stage, be patient and listen. Bring along our own interpreter if legal or technical issues are to be discussed. Present written material in both English and Chinese, using simplified Chinese characters, and be very careful that translations are accurate.

A Westerner's approach to negotiation is generally based on logical, sequential steps. For most Chinese, however, negotiation consists of a series of isolated subjects that are finally all connected together based on the value of the total deal. This approach requires persistence and can be a powerful means for Chinese negotiators to secure the point they are seeking, or at least a compromise at the very last moment.

Philippines

With a population of around 95 million people living in a complex archipelago of 710 islands, the Philippines is the 12th most populated country in the world. Nearly 92 per cent of Filipinos are of Malay origin, the remaining minorities being largely made up of groups that have visited and traded with the islands over centuries, such as Chinese, Spanish (of Mexican background) and American colonialists as well as indigenous hill tribes. Unlike other Asian countries, the vast majority of the population is Christian, mainly Roman Catholic, with a minority of Muslims living largely in the south of country.

Tagalog is the official language of the Philippines but English is generally used for educational, governmental and commercial purposes and is widely understood since it is the medium of instruction in schools. Filipinos are the third largest group of English speaking people in the world, after America and Britain. Since English is widely spoken or understood in the Philippines, it is common to hear Filipinos use a mixture of English and Tagalog words or phrases, known as 'Taglish', in daily conversation.

The Filipino family

The family is the central unit of Philippine society, underpinned by the emphasis on 'family values' of the Roman Catholic Church. The village or the *barrio* forms the community unit in which the family operates almost like a tribe. In the absence of strong central government, welfare assistance and assured employment, the family provides support and protection through its extended network of aunts, uncles, grandparents, cousins, godparents, sponsors, and close family friends.

The Filipino does not aim to obtain money and other resources for themselves but for the family group as a whole. Extended families operate like clans, often working for each other or in the same family company, sponsoring each other and sending money back to family members from the better-paid work overseas that many more qualified Filipinos are forced to undertake.

Saving or losing face

A Filipino will make great efforts to avoid shame or *hiya*. Shame may be caused by a person failing to live up to their own expectations or those of others, which means that most people seek to control their emotions and maintain a sense of social propriety. Criticizing a Filipino in public is the greatest insult (even though there is a good deal of criticism of others in private). *Hiya* makes

Filipinos fearful of failure and therefore often resistant to change or innovation.

On the other hand, self-esteem (*amor proprio*), maintenance of face and pride are highly valued. Filipinos are rather conformist and will go along with any situation rather than risk a confrontation and loss of face. A Western businessperson must recognize this and watch out for non-verbal mannerisms that will relay the (often smiling) Filipino's true feelings.

The concept of obligation and interdependency is very strong in the Philippines. A favour such as using another's business network to further a career cannot be simply repaid by money but by actions. This 'inner debt' does not have to be repaid immediately but is kept in the scale of mutual obligation for repayment at a future date.

Meeting and greeting

The American influence is strong in the Philippines, having been built up over many years of colonization and through exposure to Western movies, lifestyle and products. Many Filipinos have migrated overseas or spent considerable time working abroad. This means that they are generally more open to different cultures and ways of doing things. The widespread use of spoken English (or more often, Taglish) even on the television makes Filipinos much less narrow-minded than people in many Asian cultures and a lot less formal.

Initial greetings follow a set protocol of greeting the eldest or most important person first, but a handshake with a welcoming smile usually follows. You may be invited to use a person's first name or nickname (often Americanized like 'J.J.') but in the context of business meetings, use academic, professional, or honorific titles. Educational qualifications are much prized in the Philippines, both as marks of status and as gateways to earning money for the wider family or community.

Business cards can be printed entirely in English. Present your card first in both hands. Some senior level executives only give business cards to those of similar rank. When receiving a card, take it formally in two hands and don't slip it into a back pocket. Read it carefully, register the title, and don't write on it. Your business card should also show your job title, thereby allowing your Filipino counterparts to understand your place in your company's hierarchy. Be respectful with it.

Gifts and festivals

There are many religious festivals and saints' days in the Philippines. These may take the form of a procession or a special church service, to which the Westerner may be invited on the assumption he or she is Christian. They may also be invited to the eating and drinking that follows or to other occasions like children's christenings, birthdays and marriages. If you are invited to a Filipino home for such occasions, bring sweets (foreign chocolates such as Toblerone are highly prized), a toy for the baby or flowers for the hosts.

Avoid chrysanthemums and white lilies, since they are associated with funerals. You may send a fruit basket after the event as a thank you but not before or at the event, as it could be interpreted as meaning you do not think that the host will provide sufficient hospitality. Gifts are not supposed to be opened when received.

Dining etiquette

Dining out or at someone's home is generally more relaxed in the Philippines than elsewhere in the region. Meals are often served family-style or at buffets where you serve yourself. It usual to eat with fork and spoon and rice will be present in abundance. Hold the fork in the left hand and use it to guide food to the spoon in your right hand.

The Spanish heritage means that many Filipino males have inherited a macho attitude, which is reflected in a preference for strong liquor such a brandy or rice gin called 'GSM' (now made in a more sophisticated, lighter version for white collar professionals). Filipinos also have a wicked sense of humour and enjoy telling jokes, often at each other's expense. Be aware that in an English-speaking environment you may regret what you say when you have imbibed too freely. Filipinos appreciate handwritten notes, so send a thank you card to the hostess in the days following the meal.

Building for the long term

Due to the American influence and the use of English by many Filipinos, the country is a relatively comfortable environment in which to undertake business activities. However, care should till be taken to build long term relationships based firstly on an introduction by a Filipino known and trusted by the party you wish to meet. Filipinos are very impressed by titles and respect position, so an introduction by someone with status and a title is best.

Filipinos are very loyal once a relationship has been formed and will introduce you to further associates within their network. The principle of mutual obligation means that you may be asked to do favours for such associates, and they will expect you to ask favours from them in return. This will lead to a long-term relationship based on the balance of obligations and on your personal (rather than company) credibility. If you leave, your successor will have to build a similar network based on personal relationships.

Meetings and negotiations

Always make an appointment and arrive on time. Face-to-face meetings are preferred to other, more impersonal methods such as the telephone, fax, letter or email. The most senior person in your team should be introduced first. It may appear that negotiations are proceeding very slowly but the main purpose of the first meeting is to get to know each other as the foundation for building a further relationship. It is best not to respond with any sign of impatience or frustration.

Make sure that all your materials, client testimonials and company information have been sent in advance along with a provisional agenda. During the meeting, avoid making exaggerated claims or being pushy or boastful; modesty gets you a long way in the Philippines. Emphasise the benefits your company can offer the Filipino firm but don't expect any decisions. Given the paternalistic style of management, the decision maker may not even be there. Only the most senior people have authority and responsibility.

Since decision makers are at the top of the hierarchy, try to identify who they are and cultivate them if possible. Having contacts in high places is essential for cutting through red tape. Many bureaucrats and some business people have a *manana* attitude to life, supposedly inherited from the Spanish, and will always promise 'tomorrow'. This is backed up a by a certain fatalism, 'if it's meant to be, it will be', which is the result of centuries of enduring epidemics, floods and earthquakes.

So it is wise to factor these elements into the length of negotiations. As Filipinos are non-confrontational, they don't like saying 'no', and their 'yes' can mean all kinds of things including simply 'yes, if you say so' (hoping that if they wait for *manana*, you may well have gone home or the problem ceased to exist).

Even if a positive decision is reached, an incredibly slow and inefficient rubber stamp bureaucracy takes over with many signatures and approvals being required. It is vital not to lose your temper during this period but to find ways, preferably through your local intermediary, to expedite the process or go round the problem. Since this often includes 'tea money' or some sort of compensation, leave the intermediary to handle the required 'gift' as these delicate procedures have their own accepted rules.

Malaysia

Malaysia is split into Peninsular Malaysia, which extends from southern Thailand to Singapore, and East Malaysia, formed from the states of Sabah and Sarawak, separated by the Sultanate of Brunei on the northern coast of the island of Borneo. The population of almost 29 million people is divided into Malays (67.4 per cent), Chinese (24.6 per cent), and Indian (7.3 per cent). About 60 per cent of the population is Muslim, with the rest being Buddhist, Taoist, Christian and Hindu. Religious observance has a high priority in Malaysia, higher than any business requirements.

Bahasa Melayu is the official language, especially among Malays, but English is also commonly used. The Chinese speak the dialects of the regions of China from which they have come, or Straits Chinese, but they also widely use English. The ethnic groups retain their religions, customs and way of life and the most important festivals of each group are public holidays. The government of Malaysia is a federal parliamentary democracy of 13 states under a revolving constitutional monarchy.

The family network

Despite so much cultural diversity, Malaysians work in apparent harmony that is the result of several unifying factors. For each ethnic group, the family is considered the centre of the social structure. As a result there is a great emphasis on unity, loyalty and respect for the elderly. Leaders are often considered as 'wise elders' and their authority is unquestioned whether they are a Sultan, a headman of a village or the head of a family. Honorific terms are widely used for family members depending on their age and rank, and for members of the wider social hierarchy according to status, authority and wealth.

The family is the place where the individual can be guaranteed both emotional and financial support. When one member of the family suffers a financial setback, the rest of the family will contribute what they can to help out. This group consciousness extends into a willingness to prioritize group interest over individual concerns. Fulfilling obligations to family members, relatives, friends and the work team is extremely important. Malaysians like a team environment and a sense of belonging, and they do not find it easy to separate professional affairs from personal life.

Saving and losing face

Malays, Chinese and Indians all strive to maintain face and avoid shame both in public and private. Since employees are loyal and tend to act deferentially towards their elders and superiors, subordinates will not argue with the boss in case the latter loses face. Equally, it is not expected that the superior will show improper or coarse behavior towards subordinates. Westerners must learn to save the face of another by delaying a negative reply, not communicating negative feedback or embarrassing the other in any way. If face is preserved, interpersonal relations will be smooth and harmony and respect will be maintained.

Meeting and greeting

The three main ethnic groups are religiously and culturally diverse. This extends to meeting and greeting. Younger people or those who work in Western companies usually adopt the Western practice of shaking hands with everyone, but this may not the case with older or more reserved Malays or even Chinese. Ethnic Chinese shake hands lightly as in Hong Kong and Taiwan, although the woman must extend her hand first. Between men, ethnic Malays shake hands but men and women traditionally do not since Muslim men do not touch women in public.

These days younger Malays shake hands with both Western men and women and say *selamat*, even if it is more traditional to use a *salaam* (bowing of the head) to women. Malays may also touch their chests after shaking hands to symbolize that the greeting comes from the heart. They are pleased when the foreigner returns the gesture. Ethnic Indians shake hands with members of the same sex. Nodding of the head and smiling is more usual when being introduced to someone of the opposite sex.

Names and titles

The way names are used also varies between ethnicities:

Chinese

Chinese names in Malaysia are the same as in in the rest of the Chinese world. The surname or family name comes first, followed by two personal names. A Westerner should address a Chinese by their honorific title and their surname. If the Chinese person wants to move to a first name basis in business, they will advise you. Don't take it for granted.

Malay

Many Malays do not have surnames. Instead, men add the father's name to their own name with the connector 'bin' (son of). Sufyan Adli becomes Sufyan Adli bin Supiani. Women use the connector 'binti' (daughter of). The title Haji (male) or Hajjah (female) before the name indicates the person has made a pilgrimage to Mecca. The name Sayyed (male) or Sharifah (female) indicates that the person is considered to be a descendant of the prophet Mohammed.

Indian

Many Indians in Malaysia do not use surnames. Instead, they place the initial of their father's name in front of their own name. The man's formal name is their name 's/o' (son of) and the father's name. Women use 'd/o' to refer to themselves as the daughter of their father. Since many Indian names are extremely long, they commonly use a shortened version of their name as a sort of nickname.

Business cards

Business cards are exchanged after the initial introductions. If you are meeting a Chinese, have one side of your card translated into Chinese, with the Chinese characters printed in gold. If you are meeting government officials, have one side of your card translated into Bahasa Melayu. Present the card in both hands with the characters facing your counterpart.

Take advice on the Chinese characters for your name and title with the most auspicious connotations. When receiving a card, take it formally in two hands and don't slip it into a back pocket. Read it carefully, register the title, and don't write on it. Your business card should also show your job title, thereby allowing your Malaysian counterparts to understand your place in your company's hierarchy. Be respectful with it.

Dining etiquette

Dining etiquette is generally relaxed but depends on the setting and context. The more formal is the occasion, the more formal the behaviour. Meals are often served family-style or at buffets where you serve yourself but wait to be asked several times by the host before tucking in. Try to ask the other guests to begin before you. It is usual to eat with fork and spoon and rice will be present in abundance.

Hold the fork in the left hand and use it to guide food to the spoon in your right hand. Depending on the situation, many local guests will prefer to eat with their right hand. Don't act surprised since this is perfectly usual in Muslim countries. Make sure to pass on food dishes with your right hand only. Malaysians are rather conservative in dress. A jacket and polo shirt or a batik shirt by itself is acceptable for men. An unrevealing cotton dress that reaches the ankles and covers the neck is recommended for women.

Gifts and festivals

If you are invited to an ethnic Chinese home for dinner, take along some carefully wrapped candies or chocolate or a basket of fruit. Red and gold are auspicious colours for wrapping. Gifts can include alcohol such as plum wine for women and cognac for men, cakes and delicacies not usually found in Malaysia. At Chinese New Year, give red packets to employees, service staff at your apartment, juniors and children. Never give clocks or watches, as they are associated with death, or anything that cuts because scissors and knives suggest terminating the relationship. However, giving eight of something is considered extremely lucky. Gifts are not usually opened when received.

Ethnic Malays prefer gifts on parting rather than on arrival. Do not try to give alcohol, anything associated with pigs or pork or anything wrapped in white (the colour of death). Gifts of food should be halal. Offer gifts with the right hand or both hands. Gifts are not opened when received.

Flowers are appreciated as gifts by ethnic Indians, but avoid frangipani since it is used in funeral wreaths. Unlike for the Chinese, money should be given in odd numbers. Wrap gifts in bright colours, not in white or black. Do not give alcohol unless the recipient is known to like it. Gifts are not opened when received.

Building for the long term

As in the rest of the region, Malaysians prefer a relationship-oriented approach than a task-oriented approach. The contractual obligations of completing the job are less important than building trust. Since Malaysian communication tends to be subtle and to avoid a face-losing 'no', it is best to use the indirect conduit of a third party to deal with problems, difficulties and uncertainties.

Truth may appear to be sacrificed in the drive to preserve harmony, but in the long run harmony is preserved and hence the potential of the relationship. Bad news for either party can be more easily digested through an intermediary. Nothing will be resolved by showing frustration, anger or impatience. Malaysians will also not understand the Westerners' desire for a rapid response, thinking that it shows thoughtlessness or even rudeness. In difficult moments, they will prefer silence to speaking out, careful thought to an ill-considered reply.

Business meetings

At the first meeting between two companies, Malaysians will generally not get into in-depth discussions. They prefer to use the first meeting as an opportunity to get to know the other side and build a rapport, which is essential in this consensus-driven culture. There will be small talk about holidays and family, which should definitely avoid any reference to religion, human rights, democracy issues or the current government. Since Malaysians love rituals and ceremonies, there may well be formal speeches of welcome from all and sundry, prayers and even food. You may be required to give a short speech of thanks in return.

Decision-making is not as slow as in Japan or China, but you are unlikely to receive quick decisions. Smaller projects may come to a final decision over a few meetings that become gradually more business-intensive. Larger projects will take several meetings. Business decisions involve great attention to detail, analysis and research as well as deep thought. Every attempt is made to avoid risk, which creates a reluctance to make difficult decisions.

Much depends on your status and the standing of your company as well as the ethnic background of your counterparts. Muslim Malaysians are fatalistic, believing that a deal is meant to happen if it happens. The Chinese are more astute and decisive if a trusting relationship has been established. Some Malay business people may use shamans and fortune-tellers before coming to a conclusion, whereas a Chinese Malaysian may consult astrologers or *feng shui* experts.

Indonesia

Indonesia is a collection of over 13,500 islands, of which about half are inhabited, with an overall population of some 242 million people, the fourth largest in the world. The most heavily populated islands are Sumatra (to the west), Java (in the centre), Sulawesi, Kalimantan (southern Borneo) and Irian Jaya (western New Guinea). Most Indonesians are Muslim, with a small minority of Christians, Hindus and Buddhists. The official language is Bahasa Indonesian, a standardized dialect of the Malay language, but most people speak regional dialects such as Javanese as well as the official national language.

Each province has its own dialect, ethnic make-up, religions and history stemming from centuries-old differences in heritage, including European (largely Dutch) influences. As a result of these influences and strong local traditions, the national motto is perhaps unsurprisingly 'Unity in Diversity'.

Business people in developed countries tend to ignore Indonesia, preferring to concentrate on the vast markets of India and China. However, with a GDP growth rate of more than 6 per cent a pear and a rapidly expanding middle class, Indonesia is one of the most promising markets in the world.

Family and hierarchy

Like Malaysia, Indonesia is a collectivist culture with a traditional hierarchical and honour-oriented society. Due to the diverse nature of influences on its culture, there exists a strong pull towards the group, whether family, village or island, and loyalty towards friends and relatives of the same ethnic group and place of birth.

Families act in some ways like clans and are still very traditional in structure with hierarchical relationships being maintained. The respect shown to status, position and age is reflected both in the village and in the office where the senior person makes the important group decisions (senior persons are often called 'father' or 'mother' in the local language). Nevertheless, just like a family, all members of the group are expected to have a voice and to reach consensus after discussion.

Saving and losing face

As in Malaysia, Indonesians strive to maintain face and avoid shame (*malu*) both in public and private. Since employees are loyal and tend to act deferentially towards their elders and superiors, subordinates will not argue with the boss in case the latter loses face. Equally, it is not expected that the superior will show improper or coarse behavior towards subordinates. Westerners must learn to save the face of another by delaying a negative reply, not communicating negative feedback or embarrassing the other in any way.

Bahasa Indonesian reputedly has 12 ways of saying 'no' and several ways of saying 'yes' when 'no' is meant. If face is preserved, interpersonal relations will be smooth and harmony and respect will be maintained.

Meeting and greeting

Greetings can be rather formal as they are meant to show respect. Younger people or those who have worked in the West usually adopt the Western practice of shaking hands with everyone. Between men, Indonesians shake hands but men and women traditionally do not since Muslim men do not touch women in public. These days more cosmopolitan Indonesians shake hands with both Western men and women and say *selamat*, even if it is more traditional to use a *salaam* (bowing of the head) to women. Indonesians may also touch their chests after shaking hands to symbolize that the greeting comes from the heart. They are pleased when the foreigner returns the gesture.

Titles are important in Indonesia as they signify status. If you know someone's title ensure that you use it in conjunction with the person's name. Some Indonesians only have one name, although it is becoming more common for people to have a first name and a surname, especially in the middle class. Many Indonesians, especially those from Java, may have had an extremely long name, which has been shortened into a sort of nickname for everyday conversation. Do not use a shortened version of a name until invited to do so.

Business card etiquette is much the same as in the rest of Asia. Present the card in both hands with the Bahasa translation uppermost and the characters facing your counterpart (English is also acceptable). When receiving a card, take it formally in two hands and don't slip it into a back pocket. Read it carefully, register the title, and don't write on it. Your business card should also show your job title, thereby allowing your Indonesian counterparts to understand your place in your company's hierarchy. Be respectful with it.

Gifts and festivals

Gift giving etiquette in Indonesia heavily depends on the ethnicity of the receiver: Ethnic Malays/Muslims prefer gifts on parting rather than on arrival. Do not try to give alcohol, anything associated with pigs or pork or anything wrapped in white (the colour of death). Gifts of food should be halal. Offer gifts with the right hand or both hands. Gifts are not opened when received.

If you are invited to an ethnic Chinese home for dinner, take along some carefully wrapped candies or chocolate or a basket of fruit. Red and gold are auspicious colours for wrapping. Gifts can include alcohol such as plum wine for women and cognac for men, cakes and delicacies not usually found in Malaysia. At Chinese New Year, give red packets to employees, service staff at your apartment, juniors and children. Never give clocks or watches, as they are associated with death, or anything that cuts because scissors and knives suggest terminating the relationship. However, giving eight of something is considered extremely lucky. Gifts are not usually opened when received.

Flowers are appreciated as gifts by ethnic Indians, but avoid frangipani since it is used in funeral wreaths. Unlike for the Chinese, money should be given in odd numbers. Wrap gifts in bright colours, not in white or black. Do not give alcohol unless the recipient is known to like it. Gifts are not opened when received.

Dining etiquette
Dining etiquette is generally relaxed but depends on the setting and context. The more formal is the occasion, the more formal is the behaviour. Meals are often served family-style or at buffets where you serve yourself. Try to ask the other guests to begin before you. It is usual to eat with fork and spoon and rice will be present in abundance. Hold the fork in the left hand and use it to guide food to the spoon in your right hand. Depending on the situation, many local guests will prefer to eat

with their right hand. Don't act surprised since this is perfectly usual in Muslim countries. Make sure to pass on food dishes with your right hand only.

Indonesia, like Malaysia, is relatively conservative in dress. A jacket and polo shirt or a batik shirt by itself is acceptable for men. An unrevealing cotton dress that reaches the ankles and covers the neck is recommended for women.

Building for the long term

Personal connections are often more important than economic criteria in making business and government decisions in Indonesia. Having the right connections is extremely important since in some areas or sectors it can be very difficult to access senior people or gain a meeting without them. You therefore need a local partner who has good contacts and who can handle the commissions that may be necessary for government officials. Nevertheless, dealing with your counterpart face-to-face is eventually the most effective way of doing business in Indonesia and building a long-term relationship.

Reflecting the Malay/Islamic tradition, people who are impolite, boastful, pushy or aggressive are not respected. As in all countries in Asia, you should present yourself as polite, well mannered, sophisticated and respectful and above all show a real interest in the country, its language and culture.

Business meetings

Due to the importance of family and group within the culture, much Malay Indonesian business is conducted informally over lunches and dinners (the Chinese are more formal). Initial meetings may be more about getting-to-know-you rather than business. Do not be surprised if business is not even discussed. In Malay Indonesian culture, time is regarded as limitless (*jam karet* meaning 'rubber time'), so it should be spent with others and enjoyed. Business is therefore conducted in a very leisurely manner.

Patience is a virtue when dealing with Indonesians. Since bargaining at the market or on the street is a way of life, your best option is to join in. However, don't make concessions too quickly. Plan on a long negotiating period and allow your local partners to run the negotiations if you need to be absent. They will know the rules and be able to negotiate the appropriate government commission, which is a common aspect of doing business in Indonesia. Given the Indonesian attitude to time, 'out of sight, out of mind' will only too readily apply if no one is there to keep your company high up on your Indonesian counterpart's agenda.

Thailand

There are almost 70 million people living in Thailand, of which approximately 75 per cent are ethnic Thais. The Chinese form the largest minority with more than 14 per cent of the population, the remaining 11 per cent being made up of various ethic groups such as Malays, Mons, Khmers and refugees from Myanmar (Burma), Laos and Cambodia. The strong work ethic and family network of the Chinese, as well as inter-marriage with ethnic Thais, have ensured that they are both well integrated and successful. Chinese Thais now own several of Thailand's largest companies.

Almost 95 per cent of the population practices Theravada Buddhism. The Buddhist approach to life has strongly influenced Thai attitudes and behavior, emphasizing harmony and mutual respect, modesty, compassion for others and avoidance of conflict. *Mai pen rai* ('never mind, it doesn't matter') is a common expression in Thailand, indicating a passive attitude towards problems and a readiness to shrug off difficulties.

The Thais are very proud of their monarchy, one of the oldest in the world, and of their independence as one of the only Asian nations to have avoided Western colonization. Despite periods of military government and recurrent political turmoil, Thais also have a strong attachment to democracy and are capable of taking to the streets to defend it. Thai is largely spoken throughout the land but English is gradually becoming more prevalent in government and commerce. Thai schools also teach English as a second language.

The family and hierarchies

The family unit is the cornerstone of Thai community life and remains particularly strong in rural areas. Despite the advent of commerce and tourism, and the pursuit of material wealth, children are taught to honour their parents and elders and to depend on the extended family for mutual support.

Thais still respect hierarchical relationships. Parents are superior to their children, teachers to their students, and bosses to their subordinates. Although women usually run the family finances and are increasingly visible in Thai business and government, they still tend to be treated as secondary to men. When Thais meet a stranger, they will immediately try to place you within your own hierarchy so they know how you should be treated. This is often achieved by asking what might be regarded as very personal questions in other cultures. Don't be defensive; it is a mark of respect.

Saving and losing face

As a deeply Buddhist people, Thais place great emphasis on the outward forms of courtesy and respect. Being self-effacing, modest and not embarrassing or intruding on others is an essential part of Thai culture. In a non-confrontational society, any attempt to criticize others publicly or be openly angry amounts to an unpardonable loss of face. In such a culture, the smile is the most useful non-verbal tool and disarms as well as hides a large variety of emotions and reactions.

Thailand is known as the Land of Smiles, which indicates a good deal of relaxation and a friendly attitude but might not always be entirely positive. Make sure that you smile back and be careful not to slander or criticize the royal family in any way; it is a legal offence.

Meeting and greeting.

Thais still greet and say goodbye to each other with the traditional Buddhist greeting called the *wai*. The *wai* may be made while sitting, walking or standing. It takes the form of a slight bow forwards while bringing your hands to a praying position in front of you between chest and forehead with the fingers pointing upwards. The exact location of the hands and the depth of the bow depend on the level of respect being offered, with the junior person offering the *wai* first and the senior responding. Westerners don't have to worry about all the subtle nuances. The mere fact that you attempt a *wai* will delight your hosts. As for shaking hands, wait to see if your Thai counterpart takes the initiative. Most educated and cosmopolitan Thais now offer both a *wai* and a handshake.

Thais generally use first rather than surnames, with the honorific title 'Khun' before the name. Khun is an all purpose form of address that is appropriate for both men and women. In general, wait for your host and hostess to introduce you to the other guests. This allows everyone to understand your status relative to their own, and thus know who performs the *wai* and how low the head should be bowed.

Business cards

Business card etiquette is much the same as in the rest of Asia. Present the card in both hands with the Thai translation uppermost and the characters facing your counterpart (English is also acceptable). When receiving a card, take it formally in two hands and don't slip it into a back pocket. As in most Asian countries, it is polite to make some comment about the card, even if it is only to acknowledge the address. Read it carefully, register the title, and don't write on it. Your business card should also show your job title, thereby allowing your Thai counterparts to understand your place in your company's hierarchy. Be respectful with it.

Gifts and festivals

The Thai calendar is full of festive occasions. Once you are accepted as a long-term business partner, it is inevitable that you will be asked to attend some of these occasions. If you are invited to someone's house, take along some carefully wrapped candies or chocolate or a basket of fruit. Red and gold are suitable for both ethnic Thai and Chinese Thai households because they are royal colours.

Avoid wrapping a gift in green, black or blue as these are used at funerals and in mourning. Similarly, do not give marigolds or carnations, as they are associated with funerals. Money is the usual gift for weddings and ordination parties. Gifts are not usually opened when received.

Dining etiquette

Thais enjoy eating out and combining business with pleasure, but it is best for Westerners to wait until business issues are actually raised. The meal will almost certainly be paid for by the Thai host, so don't insist on paying yourself. Thais use chopsticks only for Chinese dishes such as noodles. In all other situations they use a fork and spoon with the spoon held in the right hand and the fork in the left. The fork is used to guide food on to the spoon.

Most meals are served as buffets or with serving platters in the centre of the table family-style. It is polite to wait to be asked if you want a second helping of anything and in a country where rice is considered sacrosanct, make sure to finish the rice in your bowl. It is equally polite not to finish everything from the service dishes, since this would imply there is not sufficient food.

Building for the long term

Business relationships develop slowly in Thailand and do not flourish after one meeting; it may take several meetings or more. Since the Thais are supportive of hierarchies and respect all forms of authority, decisions are made by senior management with little consultation of middle or junior management. The eldest person in the group is always the most revered.

If you want to build a long-term relationship, make sure that you are too are respected and are always courteous when dealing with others (the Thais call such demeanour *jai yen* or 'cool heart'). As in many Asian societies, non-verbal communication is often more important than verbal communication. You must watch your own body language and facial expressions, as these often will be believed over your words. You must also watch the non-verbal demeanour of your Thai counterparts. Remember that it is difficult for most Thais to criticize or say 'no'.

Meetings and negotiations

Always make an appointment and arrive on time. Face-to-face meetings are preferred to other, more impersonal methods such as email. The most senior person in your team should be introduced first. It may appear that negotiations are proceeding very slowly but the main purpose of the first meeting is to get to know each other as the foundation for building a further relationship. It is best not to respond with any sign of impatience or frustration.

Make sure that all your materials, client testimonials and company information have been sent in advance along with a provisional agenda. Emphasise the benefits your company can offer the Thai firm but don't expect any decisions. Given the paternalistic style of management, the decision maker may not even be there. Only the most senior people have authority and responsibility. Since decision makers are at the top of the hierarchy, try to identify who they are and cultivate them if possible. Having contacts in high places is essential for cutting through red tape.

Many business people dislike to be tied down by contracts and this is backed up by the ubiquitous and rather fatalistic *mai pen rai* ('it doesn't matter') attitude. The Thais view contracts as an early step in developing a relationship. It is better to focus on overall business objectives with an appropriate level of detail to avoid conflict and build up agreement step by step. It is also important to have an intermediary or agent to handle the issue of government 'commissions' or 'gifts' as they arise.

Vietnam

Vietnam is a densely populated country of about 88 million people, nearly 90 per cent of which are ethnic Vietnamese with the remainder being mainly ethnic Chinese. Most Vietnamese are Buddhist, but Confucianism, Taoism, animism and ancestor worship have combined to form a widely held belief system that seeks to maintain harmony within the Confucian pattern of a paternal and authoritarian society. Roman Catholicism, a legacy of French colonialism, is professed by about 10 per cent of the population.

The long and painful struggles for liberation from the Chinese, French and Americans have left the Vietnamese fiercely protective of their independence and culture. Since the government is still communist, discussions about communism and the Vietnam War are avoided in business circles. However, the Vietnamese have largely moved on from the Vietnam War and have become increasingly entrepreneurial and 'state capitalist' in recent times.

Due to their long association with colonial powers, they are less xenophobic and more cosmopolitan than many Asian countries. The success of overseas Vietnamese and their exposure to American capitalism has resulted in a general feeling of friendship for Westerners as well as a strong desire for economic success both nationally and as individuals. Modern Vietnamese aim to achieve parity with their Asian neighbors in terms of material wealth and are very brand and fashion conscious.

Confucianism and the family

The Confucian ethic still dominates family and social values in Vietnam. There is a strong sense of community and collective responsibility based on relationships within the family, on hierarchical obligations, loyalty and honour, education and learning, respect for elders and traditions, and on politeness and decorum. The extended family is still very important in rural areas, with family members contributing to the financial, social and everyday needs of the group or clan. It is not unusual for members of three generations to live under the same roof with the patriarch making the decisions for everyone.

In general, the Vietnamese are collectivists. The individual is seen as secondary to the group; whether the family, school or company. As a result there are strict guidelines for social interaction that are designed to protect a group from losing respect. The tradition of ancestor worship is as strong in Vietnam as it is in Japan or Korea, with ancestors being consulted before special family occasions such as births and weddings.

Saving or losing face

As in many other Asian nations, the concept of face is extremely important to the Vietnamese. Through their social etiquette and behaviour, Vietnamese aim to preserve a harmonious environment in which emotions remain balanced and largely hidden. This means that Vietnamese often appear helpful, polite and friendly on a personal level but they will aim to do nothing that upsets the balance or makes another person lose face.

Middle management may rarely give a straight answer or assume personal responsibility for anything. The best way to handle the question of face is not to demand 'yes-no' answers, as in Japan, and to accept the need for slow consensual decision-making.

Given Vietnam's history of subjugation, it is vital to treat Vietnamese with proper respect and to avoid any situation in whey or their country might appear to lose face. Contradicting people openly, criticizing them in front of someone else or patronizing them are a sure way to lose business. Always give face through sincere compliments and showing respect such as admiring the remarkable progress of the country.

Meeting and greeting

Greetings are formal and the oldest person is always greeted first. The Vietnamese shake hands delicately rather than bowing. Handshakes only usually take place between members of the same sex. Some Vietnamese use a two-handed shake, with the left hand on top of the right wrist. Always wait for a woman to extend her hand. If she does not, bow your head slightly.

If it's a large reception you may have to introduce yourself to the other guests but at a smaller gathering or a meeting with their team (or between both teams), wait for the host to do the honours. Use Vietnamese surnames with an honorific on first meeting. If your counterparts want to move to a first-name basis, they will advise you.

Business card etiquette is much the same as in Hong Kong and Taiwan. Present the card in both hands with the Vietnamese translation uppermost and the Roman letters facing your counterpart. When receiving a card, take it formally in two hands and don't slip it into a back pocket. Read it carefully, register the title, and don't write on it. Your business card should also show your job title, thereby allowing your Vietnamese counterparts to understand your place in your company's hierarchy. Be respectful with it.

Dining etiquette

Dining out is not a very formal experience in Vietnam, although there are certain rules of etiquette. Generally speaking, it is wise to watch what the others do and do likewise. Don't just sit down but wait to be directed to your seat. Often the foreign guest is placed in a seat of honour next to the host. Both soup spoons and chopsticks will be available next to your plate and bowl. Use the chopsticks (if you are able) to pick morsels from the various dishes and place in your bowl. Return the chopsticks to the curved rest every now and then, but don't lay them across your bowl.

Only begin eating after the host has begun and if you are offered a morsel by your host or another Vietnamese, be sure to accept it and eat it with our without rice. However, don't attempt to finish all the dishes on the table or go for a second serving and only use your spoon to drink the soup. Eating everything implies there is not enough food, quite apart from you appearing greedy. Cover you mouth with your hand if you use a toothpick.

It is rare to be invited to a Vietnamese home, which can be cramped and not very modern. But if you are invited, never refuse the invitation and follow the usual rules. Take your shoes off in the hallway and bring along elegantly wrapped gifts such as flowers, tea, coffee, fruit or incense. Don't give anything black, yellow flowers or chrysanthemums since they are associated with funerals. Enjoy the food but don't finish it all.

Building for the long term

Westerners wanting to do business in Vietnam should be aware that there are a number of power networks to circumvent in order to build a long-term relationship. The combination of a communist command economy and Confucianism means that a hierarchical and authoritative business culture is still in place, with an abundance of permissions and approvals required to do anything.

The ruling party officials are gradually giving way to the new entrepreneurs and business people in the private sector but everything still takes time. In addition to the government, Local Peoples' Committees still have their tentacles in economic activities such as local city and district investments and projects. These operate like local chieftains with their own independent kingdoms.

It is therefore essential to build alliances with them before approaching national government. While the Vietnamese entrepreneurs are practical and prepared to take more calculated risks than several other Asian neighbours, patience and local representation by someone fluent in Vietnamese and with high level contacts are essential when dealing with the various bureaucracies.

Meetings and negotiations

Business meetings are rather formal in Vietnam, with both sides often ranged opposite each other in order of precedence around a long table and the principals seated at the bottom of the U and talking across a tea table in the communist style. The most senior person should enter the room first. Remember to take your own interpreter in order to obtain a truthful account of proceedings, especially of the side conversations that often reveal more than the main exchanges.

Since the Vietnamese are mainly concerned with building the relationship first, negotiations will be slow. They will be reluctant to make decisions that could be costly if a mistake were made or to give government an excuse to intervene. An initial contract may be signed for the sake of it, even though your Vietnamese counterparts may disagree with the terms, in order to provide a jumping off point for further discussion. Business concerns come a poor second to building a lasting relationship.

The extent of technology transfer, skills development and local employee training your company offers will be the main criteria by which you and your company will be judged. Above all, you will be assessed on your long-term commitment to the country.

The undeveloped economies – Cambodia, Myanmar (Burma)

Cambodia

With a population of over 14.8 million and a land mass of 70, 000 square miles, Cambodia is one the least populous countries in Asia. The official religion is Theravada Buddhism, which is practiced by approximately 95 per cent of the Cambodian population. The country's minority groups include Vietnamese, Chinese, Chams and various hill tribes.

The kingdom is a constitutional monarchy with a parliamentary democracy. Khmer is the official language of Cambodia and is used in most social contexts including government administration, education at all levels, and in the mass media. Due to years of French colonial rule, numerous French words have been incorporated into the language. The Vietnam War extended into Cambodia and gave rise to the murderous Khmer Rouge regime. After years of isolation and civil war, the nation was reunited under the monarchy in 1993 and has seen increasing economic progress ever since.

Strong textiles, agriculture, construction, garments, and tourism sectors have attracted foreign investment and international trade. In 2005, oil and natural gas deposits were found beneath Cambodia's territorial waters, and now that commercial extraction has begun, the oil revenues are expected to significantly affect Cambodia's economy.

The family and hierarchy

The family plays a central role in Cambodia society, as in other parts of Asia, providing support and guidance to the extended family through a network of obligations presided over by the patriarch of the family. This network is backed up by the teachings of Theravada Buddhism, which reinforces a sense of hierarchy within society. Just as monks walk in order of rank, with the senior monk in front and the most junior at the rear, so too does Buddhism teach that children should pay respect to their parents, students to teachers and subordinates to managers.

This sense of hierarchy explains the personal content of many of the questions Westerners are asked on first acquaintance, such as questions about family background, company position, even relative wealth and income. Your answers to these questions may influence the way Cambodians communicate with you in future.

Saving and losing face

Cambodia is a collective society. Whether it's the family, community or company, the individual takes second place to the group. In such societies, harmonious relations are maintained through certain etiquette and protocol guidelines, such as subtle and non-verbal ways of communicating, to minimize the chances of causing offense to others or making someone lose face. Protecting both one's own and other's face is extremely important.

Given Cambodia's history of colonization and invasion, it is vital to treat Cambodians with proper respect and to avoid any situation in which they or their country might appear to lose face. Contradicting someone openly, criticizing them in front of someone else or patronizing them are a sure way to lose business. Always give face through sincere compliments, showing respect or doing something that raises self-esteem such as praising their business acumen.

Meeting and greeting
Greetings between Cambodians are dependent on the relationship, place in the hierarchy and age of the participants. The traditional greeting is similar to the Thai *wai*: a bow combined with a bringing of the hands together at chest level as if in prayer. The exact location of the hands and the depth of the bow depend on the level of respect being offered, with the junior person offering the gesture first and the senior responding.

Westerners don't have to worry about all the subtle nuances. The mere fact that you respond with the greeting you are given will delight your hosts. As for shaking hands, women may still use the traditional greeting but Cambodian men often prefer a handshake with Westerners. Cambodians generally use first rather than surnames, with the honorific title 'Lok' before a man's name and 'Lok Srey' before a woman's name.

Business card etiquette is much the same as in Hong Kong and Taiwan. Present the card in both hands with the Cambodian translation uppermost and the Khmer letters facing your counterpart. When receiving a card, take it formally in two hands and don't slip it into a back pocket. Read it carefully, register the title, and don't write on it. Your business card should also show your job title, thereby allowing your Cambodian counterparts to understand your place in your company's hierarchy. Be respectful with it.

Gifts and festivals

Gifts are usually given at Cambodian New Year. Unlike most other cultures, Cambodians do not celebrate birthdays. In fact, many older people may not know the exact date of their birth. It is rare to be invited to a Cambodian home, which can be cramped and not very modern. But if you are invited, never refuse the invitation and follow the usual rules. Take your shoes off in the hallway and bring along elegantly wrapped gifts such as flowers, tea, coffee, fruit or pastries. Don't give anything wrapped in white paper since the colour is associated with funerals. When giving a gift use both hands. Gifts are not opened when received.

Dining etiquette

Dining out is not a very formal experience in Cambodia, although there are certain rules of etiquette. Generally speaking, it is wise to watch what the others do and do likewise. Don't just sit down but wait to be directed to your seat. Often the foreign guest is placed in a seat of honour next to the host. Both soup spoons and chopsticks will be available next to your plate and bowl. Use the chopsticks (if you are able) to pick morsels from the various dishes and place in your bowl.

Return the chopsticks to the curved rest every now and then, but don't lay them across your bowl. Only begin eating after the host has begun and if you are offered a morsel by your host or another Cambodian, be sure to accept it and eat it without rice. However, don't attempt to finish all the dishes on the table or go for a second serving and only use your spoon to drink the soup. Eating everything implies there is not enough food, quite apart from you appearing greedy. Cover you mouth with your hand if you use a toothpick. Don't discuss business in social settings.

Meetings and negotiations
Business relationships develop slowly in Cambodia and do not flourish after one meeting; it may take several meetings or more. Meetings in Cambodia do not stick to an agenda. There is a certain free-for-all attitude that means that issues may be tackled separately or altogether if necessary, and once an issue has seemingly been resolved it may later be addressed again. Since Cambodians are supportive of hierarchies and respect all forms of authority, the eldest person in the group is always the most revered. If you want to build a long-term relationship, make sure that you are too are respected and are always courteous when dealing with others.

As in many Asian societies, non-verbal is often more important than verbal communication. You must watch your own body language and facial expressions, as well as those of your counterparts. For example, smiling in Cambodia (as in Thailand) is situational and can have many meanings; it may mean a person does not understand what has been said, that they are nervous or even irritated.

Cambodians prefer ideas to be brought forward in a gentle way and to wait for others to respond. Pushy, pressured or boastful communication styles have a negative effect. If Cambodians disagree with someone they would rather remain silent than make any comment. Modesty and humility are emphasized in this Buddhist culture, so compliments and praise are generally responded to by a deprecating comment. Don't expect results in the short term and always remain patient and polite.

Myanmar (Burma)

Myanmar, also known as Burma, is the second largest country in Southeast Asia with over 60 million people. The Burmans are by far the largest ethnic group with 68 per cent of the population, but there are many other ethnic groups in the country including the Shan, Karen, Rakhine, Mon, Chinese and Indian. Myanmar is a deeply Buddhist country, with 89 per cent of the population practising Buddhism and the rest holding Christian, Muslim or animist beliefs.

The official language is Burmese but English is also widely spoken by the older generation that remember the days of British colonialism (independence was declared in 1948), by school and college students that learn English in order to work as tour guides, and by business people that travel outside of Myanmar.

Since independence, the country has experienced a long-running civil war between the military government and various ethnic groups as well as an extensive period of rule by a military junta that lasted until 2011, when some form of parliamentary elections was held. Following the release of the country's main opposition leader, Aung San Sui Kyi, and her participation in the elections, a civilian government was established. However, the military continues to hold the reins of power.

Although Myanmar is a resource-rich country, the economy is one of the least developed in the world. With the lifting of sanctions by the West following Aung San Sui Kyi's release, more investment and development opportunities are opening up. But there is still a long way to go to make Myanmar, once one of the most economically advanced countries in Asia, into a developed country again.

Family and hierarchy

There is a strong sense of community and collective responsibility in Myanmar based on relationships within the family, on hierarchical obligations, loyalty and honour, education and learning. People are usually addressed according to their age. Older people's names are pre-fixed with U (pronounced Oo) and Daw, which are the equivalents of Mr. and Mrs. respectively.

A young adult is addressed by the honorifics Ko (for males) and Ma (for females). A child is referred to as Maung and Ma for males and females respectively. Generally, young people bow their head and upper body when crossing in front of old people. It's considered rude to walk in front of an older person without showing respect. Despite the widely held negative perception of the Myanmar government, most ordinary people are incredibly friendly and polite as long as you respect them and their local customs.

Saving and losing face

People with a basic knowledge of the culture of Myanmar will find it easy to live with its citizens without friction or discord. Although Myanmar's social customs are quite flexible, the ground rules are important. Harmonious relations are maintained through certain etiquette and protocol guidelines, such as subtle and non-verbal ways of communicating.

Protecting one's own and other's face is extremely important. Contradicting people openly, criticizing them in front of someone else or patronizing them are a sure way to lose friends. Always give face through sincere compliments, showing respect or doing something that raises self-esteem such as praising hospitality, admiring the beauty of Buddhist architecture or taking a genuine interest in Myanmarese traditions.

In regard to politics, avoidance of any reference to the military government, censorship, forced labour or any similar topics will not only save your counterparts' face but may possibly save them a term in prison or worse. There are still government informers on every corner and in every teashop.

Meeting and greeting

A handshake is the usual greeting between Myanmarese and Westerners, but most Myanmarese people communicate in an indirect way. Direct communication among close friends and family members is more common.

Don't be surprised if the Myanmarese offer a bow combined with a bringing of the hands together to the forehead as if in prayer when greeting a monk or an older person or on seeing an image of Buddha. The exact location of the hands and the depth of the bow depend on the level of respect being offered. As for shaking hands, women may still use the traditional greeting but Myanmarese men prefer a handshake with Westerners. A Myanmar person has no family name. A woman has her own name and retains it even after marriage.

Business card etiquette is much the same as in Cambodia or Vietnam. Present the card in both hands with the Burmese translation uppermost and the letters facing your counterpart. When receiving a card, take it formally in two hands and don't slip it into a back pocket. Read it carefully, register the title, and don't write on it. Your business card should also show your job title, thereby allowing your Burmese counterparts to understand your place in your company's hierarchy. Be respectful with it.

Gifts and festivals

Gifts are usually given at Buddhist festivals and special family occasions. It is rare to be invited to a Myanmarese home, and until recently it was even illegal for Westerners to enter private homes. But if you are invited, never refuse the invitation and follow the usual rules. Take your shoes off in the hallway and bring along elegantly wrapped gifts such as flowers, tea, coffee, fruit or pastries. Don't give anything wrapped in white paper since the colour is associated with funerals. When giving a gift use both hands. Gifts may not be opened when received.

Dining etiquette

The most commonly used tables in Myanmar are round and low and the diners have to sit on the floor or perhaps a mat during meals. Even when the table is of the international shape and height mostly used among urban families and in Myanmar restaurants, it should be small enough for the diners to reach all the dishes on the table.

All dishes including rice are served simultaneously rather than course by course. The elderly and the guests are given priority. There are no appetizers or hors d'oeuvre, and no wine or spirits served at the meal. All you can expect is drinking water, a juice or a cup of green tea. When everything is served, people can start eating, taking small portions of Myanmarese food they like. Normally, Myanmar people eat with their fingers but Myanmarese dishes are offered with serving spoons that should be handled with the clean left hand.

Soup is usually served in a single bowl for all the diners and is shared. Forks and spoons, but not knives, are permitted and have become popular. Diners intending to have another helping of rice should leave some unfinished rice on their plate as a signal that more is wanted. Rice and curry are to be eaten together rather than separately and soup can be taken at intervals. At the conclusion of the meal, Myanmar deserts such as laphet, fruit or jaggery may be served.

Dress etiquette

Myanmarese people in general cover their arms and legs. They are also courteous and considerate and low-key dress is highly appreciated, particularly in temples and monasteries (of which there are thousands). Miniskirts, shorts and sleeveless shirts are not allowed in consecrated areas, where you also have to remove your shoes. Myanmar has some of the most beautiful temples in Asia and you will be tempted to visit more than you think.

Both men and women wear a longyi, a version of the sarong that is sold everywhere. They are wrapped in different ways for men and women, so if you are adventurous (and wish to show your appreciation of local customs) find out how to tie yours; and how to keep it tied for long periods of time! For meetings, it is much safer to opt for dark cotton trousers and a long-sleeved shirt for men and a long-sleeved blouse and skirt for women.

Business meetings and negotiations

As in much of Asia, business relationships in Myanmar focus on building trust and friendship. If a business favour is received, the recipient must repay it at a later date. Business topics typically do not come up in conversation when two business people meet for the first time. Such meetings serve as an opportunity to evaluate strengths, weaknesses and personality.

Most commercial business transactions in Myanmar are carried out in English, but business cards with Burmese translation can facilitate better communication. People in Myanmar have a custom of showing respect to their elders, which means that the most senior person on both sides is expected to make all the decisions.

Negotiations take a considerable time. It is therefore essential to have a permanent representative in the country to handle all the bureaucracy, the military government 'commissions', the exchange rate issues (there is a considerable black market based on US dollars), and a private sector that is largely run by cronies and relatives of the ex-military junta. But there are considerable opportunities on the way in Myanmar and patience may be eventually rewarded.

Action Points

1. Find out everything you can about the individual country or countries in Asia where you intend to develop or are developing your business: history, population, ethnic groups, religion, and so on. Then jot down why the business etiquette, traditions and customs of this country have developed in the way they have. What are the major influences on behaviour and why are they important to your business plans?

2. List the main risks to doing business successfully in the country or countries you have chosen, especially the types of business behaviour that may easily be misunderstood or that may make your or your business counterpart lose face.

3. Consider the main differences in business etiquette and culture between Buddhist/Confucian and Muslim countries, and also the similarities.

4. If you are targeting one or more of these countries, consider hiring a coach on business etiquette, culture and negotiation/presentation skills.

5. Make sure that you have a local partner, and be ready to build a local team if you haven't done so already. Take your knowledge of the local culture into the selection process, build trust and strong partnerships based on that knowledge, and mix in local society. You can never know enough about the country where you operate.

STEP FIVE

BUILDING THE LEADERSHIP SKILLS FOR ASIA

Now that we have considered how to develop confidence through learning about the business culture and etiquette of Asia as a whole, and of individual countries in particular, it is time to address the question of performance. How will you perform within these markets? How will you gain credibility and trust with the knowledge you have acquired? How will you communicate and show leadership so that you can develop your business skills once you have overcome the initial 'entry barriers'?

The remarkable economic growth of Asia in recent decades is undoubtedly one of the most significant developments in world history. The rebalancing of global economic power towards the East continues today while Europe struggles with the aftermath of the sovereign debt crisis and America with recession and the fallout from years of high spending and low saving.

As far as we can see into the future, the high GDP growth rates, high savings ratios and increasing affluence of the developed and developing Asian economies will attract more and more Western companies to invest in the 'Asian miracle', develop pan-Asian operations and attempt to marry their business and leadership practices with those of the East.

Asian and Western models of leadership

The big question is whether those attempting to enter the Asia market for the first time have the leadership skills that are required. Are there any significant differences, for example, between the leadership styles of Asian executives and those that you are familiar with in the West? Or are they simply the result of Asian companies operating in a different culture or at a less mature stage of corporate development?

Leadership at its best is transformational. It means having a vision of the future, a strategy to reach that mission, and the ability to inspire others to reach that goal. With the widespread adoption of the MBA standard in management education throughout the world, and the rapid transfer of management techniques through the Web and international business schools, this style of leadership and its ability to transform does not differentiate the West from the East. It differentiates mediocre companies from highly successful companies all over the world.

Cultural differences

As has been shown in Step Three, cultural differences between Asian and Western economies are often a question of emphasis. For example, there are still enterprises led by family patriarchs in Western countries but they are not as common as they are in Asia. There are founder's descendants at the helm of some of America's and Europe's largest public and private companies, just as there are family dynasties heading up conglomerates in Hong Kong. Singapore, China and Malaysia. However, there are many more of them in Asia and in this sense there are some important differences in leadership style between East and West.

Professional senior managers and not family members run most Western companies. Well-managed companies have programmes for developing leaders and sophisticated succession plans. Many future leaders rise to the top through such internal programmes, although as we have seen in recent times this is not always the case. Some top executives in Western companies are parachuted into highly competitive sectors, such as investment banking, on eye-watering compensation and bonus packages.

However, Western companies are usually reliant on capital markets for their equity and debt capital (rather than directly or indirectly on government or on family wealth) and so their leaders pay more attention to stock markets than their counterparts in Asia. These stock markets tend to impose strict regulations about executive behaviour, performance and succession.

This situation is gradually changing as Asian governments tighten their regulatory regimes and corporate governance requirements, but again generally speaking, there is less freedom of action for executives and boards in the West than in Asia. It may be that Asian family firms will eventually follow the evolutionary path of Western companies towards professional management and capital obtained almost entirely from the capital markets. Several Asian countries, such as Japan, are showing progress in this direction. In the meantime, Asian companies' political and family connections continue to play a role that is far less evident or common in the West, although there are exceptions.

Leadership styles

The leadership styles evident in Asia are also less varied than in the West. The authoritarian leader that gives out the firm's direction by fiat is more common in the East, whereas the leader that relies on teamwork and participation is common in both the West and in some Asian countries like Japan. The leader that empowers and delegates to others, particularly large autonomous divisions, is gradually becoming more evident in Asia but this leadership style is far more common in Western companies. Overall, adaptability is less common and less valued in Asia than in the West.

These are important points to bear in mind. But as you develop your business in Asia, this apparent 'conservatism' should not discourage you. Information technology and the internet are bringing out a type of leadership that is becoming rapidly more evident in the East: entrepreneurial, innovative and ambitious.

Take Dr Victor Fung of Li & Fung, a traditional Chinese family-owned trading company in Hong Kong. Victor Fung was educated at Harvard University. He also works within the close-knit Chinese world of relationships. His company uses technology to obtain maximum efficiency from the global supply chain, handling every stage of the process from raw material to manufacturing high-demand consumer goods at a much lower cost than in the West. In many ways Victor Fung is an old-style Chinese taipan. But he is also a sophisticated,

Western-style technocrat capable of communicating his leadership style and business techniques to a global audience. As such he represents the new style of Asian leader. The question is whether this type of leadership will eventually become the principal or even the only one in Asia.

Clearly, Asian companies will gradually come to rely more on professional employees and professional services than they do today. In the process, it is likely that a less autocratic and more participative style of leadership will emerge to resemble that of the West. Even so, significant cultural differences will remain.

Communicating across cultures

For this reason, every newcomer to the Asian business world must learn the art of cross-cultural communication. As we have seen, in Asia's high context cultures, where mutual trust and understanding are the essential pre-requisites to building successful partnerships, much emphasis is placed on correct behaviour, awareness of position and knowledge of local customs.

For the Western businessman used to selling products and services through tightly focused presentations or in direct negotiations that have clear goals and outcomes, communication is based largely on the lingua franca of English. The message in English is usually expressed in bullet points, Powerpoint slides, videos and factual material provided by sales and marketing, finance or other relevant departments. In larger companies, a Western CEO or Chairman may give the occasional speech in English at prestigious local seminars, openings and launches, as well as at international conferences in order to maintain and develop the company's reputation and brand.

However, in Asia the cultural context of the speech or presentation is just as important as is knowledge of local etiquette and customs when attending a business dinner. It is true that the business lingua franca of Asia is English, and much of the internet and even cross-cultural e-mail communication is based on English. But a one-size-fits-all English presentation for Asia is unlikely to succeed. Every presentation must be coloured by local references, by knowledge of national or religious customs, and by sensitivity to the business culture of the country in question.

As a speechwriter, I learned never to write exactly the same speech or presentation to be given in Tokyo or Kuala Lumpur, Seoul or Singapore. The local context not only adds flavour to a speech, but it also determines whether the speech is successful or not.

A Westerner giving a presentation in Malaysia should be reasonably informed about Islam, have some knowledge of the ethnic mix of Malays and Chinese in Malaysia, and might be aware that Sharia law has influenced the marketing of certain products in the Malaysian market. A Westerner speaking in Hong Kong should be aware of the importance of Chinese New Year or of the colour red for prosperity or the lucky number eight, which the Chinese try to include in their phone numbers, passports and addresses.

These are simple examples. In many ways it doesn't matter so much *what* Westerners know about local culture. It is important that they show they know *something*. For that something will give them an entrée to the business circles they are attempting to penetrate.

Local language

Knowledge of the local language is also important. In an era of 24/7 global communications, of texting and social media, it would be easy to assume that the English language united the people of the world and that is all that a Western business executive needs. However, in almost every Asian country outside Australia and New Zealand, the opposite is true: English is the second language, a language used in business only when interfacing with foreigners, while the national language and a host of accompanying dialects are the predominant means of communication.

It is remarkable when travelling in Asian countries how readily smiles appear and doors open when a Westerner speaks a phrase in Thai or Korean, Chinese or Japanese. Often it is enough to know the words for 'good morning' and 'good evening' or 'how are you/fine thank you' in the local language for an extra level of respect and warmth to be added to the relationship.

I was once in a lift in Manila and guessed that the suited man next to me was probably a Korean. He had a Filipino bodyguard and looked important, indeed intimidating. He turned his head and looked hard at me. Not sure how to respond, I blurted out 'anyong haseyo' ('good morning' in Korean). The man's face crumpled in pleasure. We started chatting and he told me he was from Gangnam in Seoul, to which I replied 'Ah, home of the Orange Set.' This pleased him even more, 'Orange Set' being the 1990s name of the movers and shakers that live and work in Gangnam (recently satirised in PSY's 'Gangnam Style'). He couldn't understand how I knew about Korean life. Before long he had invited me to dinner where he offered me a job writing English presentations about his company for audiences all over the world. That's just one example of how far a little local language (and knowledge) can get you in Asia.

So if this is true while travelling, imagine how much more valuable those few words are in the context of a business dinner, a home invitation or when added to speeches, presentations and internal communications. Unless you are a polymath, it is not necessary to learn Thai or Japanese or Chinese in any depth. Your representative or members of your team can communicate for you when fluency is required. But an occasional phrase (perhaps just two words) or knowledge of a local expression dropped into a text can generate that essential rapport between audience and speaker that make a sales presentation or a keynote speech equally memorable.

How am I perceived?

In high context cultures, perception is as important, perhaps even more important than what is said. If the way you communicate comes over as lecturing or careless of where you are or whom you are talking to (the one-size-fits-all syndrome), your audience will not warm to you. If on the other hand you show awareness of the cultural diversity or ethnic backgrounds of your audience, you will gain respect and support for the message you are aiming to convey.

Remember that your Asian audience may well be formulating responses to you or your message in the silences and pauses in your presentation, even when being asked a question, rather than in the more obviously amusing or applause-worthy sections. So be prepared to be scrutinized and adapt your words, your timing, and your body language accordingly. Don't run around the stage or over-compensate with lots of gestures. Be cool, take stock, and allow a pause for a 'foreign' or unusual thought to be registered.

All cultures are slightly different, and Asian cultures perhaps even more so. So try to allow a moment for your message or your joke to be mentally translated and digested, even when it's accompanied (as it should be) with the occasional local reference to make it more palatable. Above all, remember that Asians have their own first languages and will need clarity of enunciation, as well as clear, simple and brief messages in English to absorb whatever you want to say.

Asians are great storytellers, so go ahead and tell a good story with the time-hallowed 'Beginning, Middle and End' structure. Announce what you want to say (a clear and unique message), develop that message with any qualifications and challenges and cross-currents you consider necessary, return to the main message. Or to put it another way: announce what you're going to say, say it, and tell them that you've said it. Finish off with some memorable uplift and/or phrase. And if you really want to ensure that you get through, use the very latest technology in all your presentations.

Asians are technology geeks to the hilt, and they possess the very latest in smartphone, PDA, videoconferencing and voice interactive tools and gadgets. They are fanatical about the latest technology, so make sure you don't roll out the old Powerpoint slides with an overhead projector and a faulty microphone.

Building successful cross-cultural teams

Successful cross-cultural communications build successful cross-cultural teams. Politically, socially or religiously sensitive issues that have the potential to offend your counterparts or hosts or other members of the local team you have assembled should be avoided. Unifying cultural experiences, such as a shared sense of humour and a belief in the value of teamwork and cohesiveness, should be highlighted.

Generally speaking, you should try to implement the principle of diversity and inclusiveness in the way you do business in Asia. As ambassadors both for your companies and for the countries where you originate, you should show cultural sensitivity as soon as you arrive and try to develop a network of trusted business associates and a local team that reflects the country's ethnic and religious diversity.

In some countries you will find yourself dealing with more than one ethnic group as well as expatriates. You will have to find a way of showing sensitivity to the needs of each of these groups. A strong team spirit and work ethic can be developed from such different elements, as well as enduring relationships with the local business network. Westerners that are able to build a reputation of being fair-minded and inclusive will usually succeed in winning people over in Asia, whereas those with a manipulative or authoritarian or condescending style will damage mutual trust.

Action Points

1. Jot down what you consider your own leadership style or way of doing things, and then compare this with any experience you have had of Asian companies. Are there any significant differences, or is it simply a matter of emphasis and perception?

2. Imagine that you have to give a speech or presentation about your business in three Asian capital cities. Write down what you might add to the speech to give it a little more local colour, or to get the (largely local) audience on your side. Try to choose cities that are known for being quite different.

3. Map out a three-part story of your product or business line with a Beginning, Middle and End. Locate what the one key message or takeaway will be and where you will place it and repeat it for maximum impact.

4. Consider what are the most sensitive issues in the Asian market (s) where you operate and how you might avoid them or show you that you recognize them in the way that you build your teams, choose partners and show leadership.

5. Write down what you see as the driving values of the local culture and map out how you could incorporate them into a speech or presentation about your company, brand or product.

STEP SIX

THE ROAD MAP TO GREATER SUCCESS

The road to doing business in Asia is challenging but it is undoubtedly worth the effort. If you want to grow your confidence, your business and your brand in Asia you must follow the steps set out in this book, developing your knowledge and mind-set as you go along. That is the Asian way of doing things. If you can learn to listen and not assert yourself continually, to observe and accept traditions and behaviours that may often seem oblique and even time wasting, to be patient and not expect immediate rewards, you will be on your way to becoming an accepted, long-term partner in the Asian business world.

Whether you are a business owner, entrepreneur, JV partner, new subsidiary of a Western company, or operating in any other line of business, the only way to unlock Asian markets is by taking the kind of step-by-step approach outlined in this book. This book is not the end of the learning process. It is the beginning of it.

As outlined in Step Four, each country has its own traditions and requires a different focus. Once you have mentally conquered the six steps of this book, you will have the required knowledge to put your knowledge into action and to tackle the subtleties of business and social behaviour that are unique to your market. But to really develop your business, you will have to go further. You will have to deepen that knowledge.

There is no short cut to business success in Asia. You will need to IMMERSE yourself in the history and culture of the country where you expect to set up, expand or build a permanent presence. This immersion is not achievable in a day, or a week, but requires constant attention and a genuine interest, indeed passion. I recently heard a senior trade official from the West say on return from Asia, 'you have to go back to being a child: inquisitive, curious, watching and learning, play-acting and role-playing.' That's exactly the mind-set.

The sooner you can drop local topics, religious festivals or 'contemporary' topics into your business conversation, for example, the sooner that all-important trust will be built. Politics is the exception to this rule. Don't get involved in any political discussion or comments about the government (you don't always know who is at your or at the next table). On the other hand, be ready to enter with relish into the daily life, customs, religious and family festivals, business entertaining, and all the other aspects of the local culture of the country in which you are operating or intend to operate.

Remember the essential '4 Ps' of doing business in Asia, and if necessary place them up on your office wall to remind yourself of their importance:

- **P**atience (credibility and trust are key in Asia and they cannot be built overnight or even in a couple of years)

- **P**resence (you must be there on a regular basis, always contactable in person, the face and the presence of your company)

- **P**resentation (you must tailor your behaviour, communications and 'personal branding' to your Asian audience)

- **P**erspective (you must see things from the viewpoint of someone with another background, in a different business, social and religious culture to your own)

Consideration and respect should be at the heart of everything you do, and remember that small gestures can often be as important as large ones. Observe how local people behave, what they wear, how they greet one another, how they eat. If you follow their example, you will build business relationships and friendships that last a lifetime.

Travel and cultural resources

Nowadays, there are plenty of business books on individual Asian countries, but most of them are academic and conceptual. Some of them are hard going. Many focus almost entirely on business management styles, legal, tax and regulatory issues. These are obviously important issues and will need to be studied by you or your staff or your consultant at the very earliest stage. However, in addition to these essential 'hardware' guides, cultural 'software' in the form of a good contemporary travel book (preferably full of personal experience), and some books on how best to travel in and enjoy the country in question are recommended.

An introduction to the language, with some simple phrases, is also useful even if you are largely employing local people. If you as a Westerner can say *Anyong haseyo* (Good morning) in South Korea or *Gay ho ma* (How are you?) in Hong Kong, your company is already on the road to being accepted. In largely Muslim or Buddhist countries (90 per cent of Asia countries beyond India, excluding Australia and New Zealand), some knowledge of religious beliefs is also required, if only to say that you have visited a temple or mosque and been favourably impressed – you even remembered to take off your shoes at the required place!

Many business people come to Asia with a readiness to learn, but just as many (and perhaps more) come with a mind-set that is still firmly rooted in their own countries in what is loosely called 'the West'. North Americans, Europeans, Australians and New Zealanders often find in the Asian country where they are posted or where they are attempting to set up and expand their business a ready-made expatriate world (often a defined area of living and relaxing and entertaining) where their Western habits of thought and behaviour are supported and encouraged.

Many of those employed by multinational companies never attempt to step outside this world into the local culture, or bother to find out what makes their Asian work colleagues or business partners and prospects tick. Some stick fondly to the belief that Western ways of doing things are somehow 'superior' to the etiquette, beliefs and traditions of the culture in which they find themselves.

This attitude is easily supported by the ubiquity of the internet, social media and of spoken English. However, although this modus operandi may be fine for those expecting a temporary posting, for anyone wanting to seriously do business in China, Indonesia, Japan, Korea or any other Asian country, such an approach is not only short sighted but also actively damaging to business prospects.

If you want to find out about the country that you are targeting, both beforehand and while you are there, by all means use the seasoned advice of experienced expatriates and also the internet to find out about the local business etiquette and culture (I have included some useful links in the section that follows). But also find out about and experience the culture itself, not through the optic of other Western expats but through local people. They are your greatest resource and source of information.

There is a rich seam of travel literature about individual Asian countries, and many books of personal experience by Western writers while trekking, searching for some lost destination, exploring off the beaten track, finding the heart of a city or living together with Asian peoples. Pilgrimages, odysseys, quests, confessions, discoveries: all these and more have created a fascinating tradition of Western travel writing on Asia.

Find books about Asian cuisine too, about Buddhism and Islam, about history and invasions, about the Japanese samurai and Chinese kung fu masters. Anything that adds to your understanding of the country or countries where you want to establish or expand your business will add a vital extra dimension to your business skills and hence prospects.

If you really immerse yourself, you may find – as I do – that you cannot avoid being tempted by the Chinese or Japanese movie on your long-haul flight to the East, that you really want to find out what is in that strange-looking steel bowl of rice and vegetables topped by a fried egg and a slick of chilli paste in the local Korean restaurant. In this case, a little knowledge is not a dangerous thing. It is essential for doing business in Asia.

In order to help you prepare a mental checklist and map out an initial plan of action, I have listed below a summary of the most important action points from this book:

12 Action Points – Summary

1. Find out everything you can about the society in which you plan to operate: the principle religion or beliefs (Confucianism, Buddhism or Islam), the nuances of respect and hierarchy, the attitude to harmony and 'collectivism' and family values, even the attitude to time and punctuality.

2. Research whether the business models you encounter will be influenced by non-economic issues such as religion, family ownership and other loyalty structures. Take advice from experienced expats, as well as from local Thais, Malaysians, Singaporeans, and so on.

3. Be aware of the importance and etiquette of business card exchange in Asia. Make sure all your details are on the card and that English is printed on one side and the local language on the other. Always have an

abundant stock of business cards. Practise the art of politely giving and receiving business cards with a colleague.

4. Inform yourself fully on the negotiation practices in the country, the incidence of corruption, and the habits of 'gifts' or 'commissions' that you or your representative will have to navigate.

5. Try to come to terms with the concept of 'face' (giving, saving and losing it), which is essential in dealing with Asians. Avoid putting possible clients and partners in 'yes-no' situations, and expect oblique answers as part of the process of creating a relationship.

6. Prepare yourself for attendance at local festivals and business dinners by learning what to give as gifts, what not to give as gifts, how to behave at banquets and home visits, and how not to give offence but to be a celebrated guest.

7. Give yourself face by presenting letters of introduction from business leaders (local or expatriate) known to your hosts, overseas members of the local business community, and former government officials who have dealt with the country.

8. Provide precise and clear written information in both English and the local language (s) on your company, your proposal and what your clients have said about you for use at the initial meetings and beforehand.

9. Be ready to build up a network of relationships that will bear fruit in the long term rather than the short term.

10. Rather than try to learn Japanese or Chinese or Thai in any depth, pick up some simple local phrases and expressions that can be dropped into conversation as an ice-breaker: such as normal courtesies and greetings, as well as an occasional saying that everyone will recognize.

11. In presentations or meetings, be prepared to be scrutinized and adapt your words, your timing and your body language accordingly. Learn to expect silences and pauses for your words to be digested. Always make sure to present yourself well in all senses and that your 'personal branding' is top-class.

12. Show cultural sensitivity and build up a network of business associates and a local team that reflects the country's ethnic and religious diversity. Demonstrate fair-mindedness and inclusivity at all times.

Congratulations! You have reached the end of this 6-step *Master Key to Asia*. I hope that the points made in the book will help you as you develop your business in Asia and I look forward to hearing from you on your progress and how I can be of further service to you.

Remember, this is just the beginning of the journey. There is no quick recipe for success in Asia, because everything is built on trust and credibility and long-term relationships. There are more than 21 countries and cultures to consider and navigate. Your progress may be fast or slow depending on which one (s) you choose and how deeply you want to engage.

I have listed below some links to books on Asia that I have found especially helpful or interesting as 'master keys' to the countries and cultures of the East. I have also added links to some of my own books that I have written while being on the road as a travel writer in business class (or a businessman in coach class). They can be found in more detail at www.davidcliveprice.com/booksonasia.

All these books are simply suggestive of the fascinating diversity and richness of life in Asia, which you as a businessperson will be able to explore, enjoy and harness to build long-term relationships and reap future business rewards. I hope you find them useful and I wish you the greatest success!

David Clive Price
International Cultural Expert
& Revenue Growth Strategist
www.davidcliveprice.com

www.facebook.com/davidcliveprice

www.twitter.com/davidcliveprice

For questions and enquiries, e-mail
david@davidcliveprice.com

RESOURCES AND LINKS

What's Next?
Your Free Gift 'Asian Communication and Culture Cheat Sheet' http://davidcliveprice.com/the-master-key-to-asia-book-gift/

Ask *The Master Key to Asia* coach a question by e-mail david@davidcliveprice.com

Useful Links

* http://www.goodreads.com/list/show/1144. Best_books_on_Asia

* http://www.southeastasiabackpacker.com/10-most-popular-backpacker-books-in-south-east-asia

* http://www.agimag.co.uk/top-10-books-on-asia-from-2012/

* http://www.amazon.com/Best-Sellers-Books-Asian-Travel-Guides/zgbs/books/16772

* http://www.amazon.co.uk/Best-Business-Books-Asia/lm/2ZPPFTB06ZV7E

* http://www.ranker.com/list/books-about-the-subject-southeast-asia/reference

* http://www.cnn.co.uk/ASIANOW/media.sites.html

Selected Books

- *The Traveler's Guide to Asian Customs and Manners*, Elizabeth Devine and Nancy L. Braganti, St. Martin's Griffin 1998

- *Chinese Business Etiquette, The Practical Pocket Guide*, Stefan H.Verstappen, Stone Bridge Press 2008

- *Kiss, Bow, or Shake Hands Asia*, Terri Morrison and Wayne A. Conway, Adams Media 2007

- *Asian Business Customs and Manners*, Mary Murray Bosrock, Meadowbrook Press 2007

- *Asian Ways, A Westerner's Guide to Asian Business Etiquette*, Nick French, Aardvark Press 2008

- *Live & Work in China & Hong Kong*, Jocelyn Kan and Hakwan Lau, Crimson Publishing 2008

- *Culture + Business in Asia*, Maureen Girdham, Palgrave Macmillan 2009

DAVID CLIVE PRICE

DAVID CLIVE PRICE has had a passion for Asia's peoples and cultures ever since he went to Japan in the 1980s and wrote a book about his travels throughout the country. This passion developed further in Hong Kong, where he struggled to make ends meet as a writer in the 1990s, wrote economic reports about Asian countries, and travelled all over the region researching books and articles. Finding himself on his pin ends with his Chinese spouse in a walk-up one-room apartment above a nightclub in Hong Kong, he resolved to join the corporate world and became Executive Speechwriter for Asia for one of the world's leading banks. It was 1995. Hong Kong was preparing to return to China. David spent the next few years writing speeches to be given by business and political leaders all over Asia and the world. He also began publishing a series of books on South Korea, Hong Kong, China, India, and Buddhism in the daily life of Asia.

In 2000, he set up his own consultancy advising Asian multinationals and Western companies with Asian operations on their strategies and communications for cross-border expansion. This experience, and the challenges he faced launching his own business, forms the basis of his Master Key Series™ on the business cultures of Asia's high-growth markets.

Check out his blog posts and articles at www.davidcliveprice.com and his daily posts on Facebook, Twitter and LinkedIn.

MORE BOOKS FROM THE AUTHOR IN THE MASTER KEY SERIES™

The Master Key to China

The Master Key to Japan

The Master Key to Malaysia

The Master Key to Thailand

The Master Key to South Korea

CONTACT INFORMATION AND OTHER PRODUCTS AND SERVICES

If you believe your friends and colleagues would get something valuable out of this book, I'd be honoured if you post your thoughts on www.facebook.com/davidcliveprice or recommend the book on Twitter and LinkedIn.

If you feel particularly strongly about the contributions this book made to your business in Asia, I'd be very grateful if you posted a review on Amazon. Any points raised or questions you would like to pursue can be sent to me directly at david@davidcliveprice.com.

Finally, if you want to go further and deeper into individual Asian markets, you can find detailed information on my International Business Passport™ keynote programmes and the Master Key Series™ at my website, www.davidcliveprice.com.

www.ingramcontent.com/pod-product-compliance
Lightning Source LLC
Chambersburg PA
CBHW030941210326
41519CB00045B/3684